MW00352724

DANDI SWAMI

— ★ —

The Story of the Guru's Will,
Maharishi Mahesh Yogi,
the Shankaracharyas
of Jyotir Math,
&
Meetings with
Dandi Swami Narayananand Saraswati

Compiled by
Paul Mason

Titles by Paul Mason:

Via Rishikesh: A Hitch-Hiker's Tale

The Maharishi:
The Biography of the Man Who Gave Transcendental Meditation to the World
Element Books – First English edition 1994

Evolution Books – Revised English edition 2005

Maharishi Mahesh Yogi - Aquamarin Verlag – German edition 1995)

O Maharishi - Nova Era – Portuguese editon 1997

Mala: A String of Unexpected Meetings

108 Discourses of Guru Dev:
The Life and Teachings of Swami Brahmananda Saraswati,
Shankaracharya of Jyotirmath (1941-53) Volume I

The Biography of Guru Dev:
The Life and Teachings of Swami Brahmananda Saraswati,
Shankaracharya of Jyotirmath (1941-53) - Volume II

Guru Dev as Presented by Maharishi Mahesh Yogi:
The Life and Teachings of Swami Brahmananda Saraswati,
Shankaracharya of Jyotirmath (1941-53) - Volume III

Kathy's Story

The Knack of Meditation

Dandi Swami

Paul Mason learned the technique of Transcendental Meditation in 1970 when he visited the Maharishi's *ashram* at Rishikesh after having hitchhiked to India. This spurred him to dig deeper into the history of the teaching of meditation, which led to his being commissioned to write the biography of Maharishi Mahesh Yogi - published in 1994 as *'The Maharishi: the Biography of the Man Who Gave Transcendental Meditation to the World'*. Later he would translate the teachings and life story of Guru Dev, Shankaracharya Swami Brahmananda Saraswati, from Hindi and Sanskrit into English.

Paul was given the honorary *sannyasi* name of 'Premanand' at Swargashram in 2000.

PREMANAND
premanandpaul@yahoo.co.uk
www.paulmason.info

© Paul Mason 2014
First published by Premanand 2014
ISBN: 978-0-9562228-4-8

Cover design by Premanand

Foreword

Initially, the idea is for a short video, a sequence of photographs, as a tribute to the memory of Dandi Swami Narayananand Saraswati, for the likes of Tony Evenson and others who never got to meet Dandi Swami. But instead of being used to make a video, the photos are instead used to create several webpages, which are still online.

Then it emerges that Rob H. van Dijk published an account of his meetings with Dandi Swami, so the race is on to find a copy. Only to find it is written in Dutch with no English version available! At first this setback seems insurmountable, that is until Manon van Dijk of Viveki Publishers sends me a machine-readable copy of *'Op zoek in India'* and suggests using Google Translate. A great idea, but though it gives glimpses of Rob's account, much of the text becomes mangled and garbled. However, help is at hand, with Paul van Oyen offering to translate Rob's meetings with Dandi Swami - brilliant, bravo! Paul then makes some useful suggestions about additional content. Rob's publisher is also very helpful, providing further information and photographs.

At the time I met Dandi Swami, he was living in a stone hut set amongst the disused buildings of the former Academy of Meditation, the *ashram* where The Beatles famously stayed back in 1968. So, it seems appropriate to include some background information about Maharishi Mahesh Yogi, who brought Transcendental Meditation to the western world, and to say something of his Master, 'Guru Dev', Shankaracharya of Jyotir Math, and his disciples.

Well... big, big thanks, to Rob van Dijk for his legacy of recollections and photographs. Thanks to Bjarne, Randy, Gunnar, Dana, Paul Saltzman and everyone else whose photographs are included. Thanks to those who shared their personal accounts, and thanks to David Sieveking for sending the sound files of his interviews in India. Thanks also to Declan Fitzmaurice for his input, and to John Reigstad for his invaluable assistance in helping to de-glitch the text.

Thanks naturally go to Kathy (big round of applause) for giving me space, understanding and support whilst getting this project accomplished.

Contents

1.	Shankaracharya Swami Brahmanand Saraswati	9
2.	The Guru's Will	23
3.	Maharishi Mahesh Yogi and Shankaracharya Swami Shantanand	31
4.	The Beatles, Rishikesh, Jyotir Math and Uttar Kashi	41
5.	Darshan of Dandi Swami Narayanananda Saraswati	65
6.	Dandi Swami and Rob van Dijk	77
7.	Dandi Swami and Paul Mason	85
8.	Air Letter to Maharishi	93
9.	Rob van Dijk Returns to Dandi Swami	95
10.	Dandi Swami Surprises	123
11.	A New Kutir for Dandi Swami	129
12.	More Visitors for Dandi Swami's Darshan	139
13.	The Passing of Maharishi Mahesh Yogi	147
14.	David Sieveking interviews the Shankaracharya of Dwaraka	149
15	David Sieveking interviews Dandi Swami Narayananand Saraswati	153
16.	In Silence Until Kumbha Mela	161

- 1 -

Painting at Jyotir Math Ashram

Adi Shankara is said to have been an ascetic who revived and reformed the national religion of India. He is understood to have been born at Kaladi in the Chera Kingdom, (situated in modern Kerala). At the age of eight years old, Shankara was initiated as a *sannyasi* (monk).

Adi Shankara is famous for having meditated in a Himalayan cave, and for having set up a monastery (also known as a *math* or *peeth*). His four disciples, Padmapada, Hasta Malaka, Trotakacharya and Sureshwara, were assigned to oversee *maths* at Govardhan in the east, Dwaraka in the west, Jyotir Math in the North and Sringeri in the south. Shankaracharya Adi Shankara died at the age of thirty-three.

The title 'Shankaracharya' is formed from the name 'Shankara' and the word '*acharya*' - Shankar is the name of the god Shiva and also the name of Adi Shankara (and '*adi*' has a meaning of 'first' or 'original') and '*acharya*' simply means 'teacher'. Each '*math*', or monastery, has its own *parampara* (succession) leading back to Adi Shankara, and every new head of a *math* is known as 'Shankaracharya'. Perhaps this is why there is confusion as to when Shankaracharya lived – with recorded dates of birth ranging from 507 BC - 805 AD.

Bhagwan Mahesh Shiva Shankar
Lord of Yogis
Portrait Painting at Jyotir Math Ashram

The Shankaracharya is believed by some to be a living incarnation of god Shiva - Shiva Shankar, Lord of *yogis* - and supposedly incapable of speaking untruth.

* * * * *

In 1940, in a new spirit of revivalism, a society known as 'Bharat Dharma Mahamandal', 'The All-India Dharma Association', discusses the idea of restoring the northern seat of Shankaracharya, which has traditionally been situated at Jyotir Math in a remote region of the Himalayas, in Northwest India, close to the Tibetan border. The seat is thought to have been vacant for over 150 years.

Shankaracharya Swami Brahmanand Saraswati, Varanasi 1941

A reclusive monk, renowned for his piety and learning, is approached to take this venerated position and on Tuesday 1st April 1941, at Shri Brahma Niwas Ashram in Siddhigiri Bhag, Varanasi, to the east of India, near Calcutta, Swami Brahmanand Saraswati is ordained as Shankaracharya of Jyotir Math.

From the *gaddi* (throne) of Shankaracharya, Swami Brahmanand sets about spreading the message of Adi Shankara, the teachings of *sanatan dharma*, which entails him in a great amount of traveling throughout north and central India. As Shankaracharya he has also to organise the re-building of the monastery of Jyotir Math, at the township of Joshimath, in an inaccessible region of the Himalayas in fairly close proximity to the ancient venerated temples of Badrinath and Kedarnath. Wherever he visits he is worshipped, and the crowds of faithful folk listen to his short lectures attentively.

At the cease to hostilities after World War II, Swami Brahmananda is asked his view of this victory. Here is a small extract of his reply: - *'Up to what extent can we suppress our outer enemies? We subdue one but are intimidated by another, this then is the suppression of an enemy but there is no sign of triumph. Whilst victory over the internal enemies is not obtained then this will remain the condition. Therefore, this much is necessary, that the leader of a country obtains triumph over his own inner antarika shadarivarga (group of six inner enemies viz. 'kaama' lust, 'krodha' anger, 'lobha' greed, 'moha' delusion, 'mada' intoxification and 'maatsarya' jealousy). Thus if the leader of society is really victorious, then they can successfully demonstrate the path of lasting happiness and peace for the country and the whole world.'* – *'Shri Shankaracharya Vaksudha'*

श्री १००८ दण्डी स्वामी
अद्वैतानन्द सरस्वती जी महाराज हिमालयवासी

Shri 1008 Dandi Swami Adwaitanand Saraswati

In 1947, a book on the life and teachings of Shankaracharya Swami Brahmanand Saraswati is published by the *ashram,* entitled; *'Shri Shankaracharya Vaksudha - Pratham Bhag', 'The Nectar Words of Shri Shankaracharya - Part One'*. The Hindi paperback is priced at three rupees, printed by the Narmada Printing Press at Jabalpur, and attributed to Shri 108 Dandi Swami Adwaitanand Saraswati, with introduction, compilation and editing credited to one 'Shri Mahesh Prasad ji'.

Shankaracharya Swami Brahmanand Saraswati
at Bandha, near Bheraghat, Jabalpur M.P. India, Guru Purnima day, July 3rd 1947
right of *guru*, Swami Karpatri with *chamara*, white whisk, then Pandit Shri Dwarika Prasad Shastri Ji,
& far right, Shri Jugal Kishor Shrivastava
Seated front left, holding Lord Shiva's *trishul* or trident, is 'Revolutionary Sadhu' Pothiram Upadhyay
Photograph courtesy of Shri Umesh Shrivastava

'We never say to accept our words; because if you will accept our own personal statement, then you will be in the habit of accepting the words of the Shankaracharya. Then, if anyone unfit is coming on the throne, then you will accept his words too. From any personal notions there will be no welfare, welfare then, will be from accepting the words of the Veda Shastra. Therefore we say; "Don't get the habit of accepting the personal views of the Shankaracharya, accept what is said according to the Veda Shastra. The Shastra is said to be the command of Bhagwan." - 'Shri Shankaracharya Upadeshamrit', '108 Discourses of Guru Dev'

'We are told the "yoga" of stopping the fluctuations of consciousness. The ultimate aim is this, that by the practice of having stopped the fluctuations of the inner self, to experience the Supreme form of the Self. Calm without a wave in any part of the pool of water, that manner a person can see his own face. That really is the method, stopping the fluctuations of the consciousness is really giving a clear reflection of the imperishable Self in the instrument of inner vision. This indeed is "darshan" (sight) of "atma" (self or soul).' - 'Shri Shankaracharya Vaksudha'

The secretary of the Shankaracharya *ashram* in Varanasi is a man in his mid-to-late twenties, known as Mahesh Ji, who is said to be the son of a tax inspector, university educated, and previously engaged as a lowly paid clerk, in the Gun Carriage Factory at Jabalpur, central India.

"Right in the beginning, I joined the ashram, I came, and then I was amongst thirty or forty brahmacharis, and pandits and all that, all that. And they were very wise people, pandits of all the six systems of philosophy, and pandits of all the smrittis, shrutis, and all that. The whole learning round about Shankaracharya was a vast retinue of learned people and I was absolutely insignificant. I had some knowledge of Hindi, and some of English, and a little bit of Sanskrit, but in that big huge learned assembly, this was absolutely insignificant, and English, of course, it was not necessary at all.

And then it was about a week and as everyone in the morning would go and do the prostrations and come out, and then there was nothing to do. And one week passed, and then I thought. "It's ridiculous to waste all this time." Was just once in the morning and once in the evening, go and prostrate and come out. So I made friends with a man who was cleaning his room, something like that, like that. Adjusting his table, this, this, this.

I said, "Oh, could you not take rest? You must be feeling very tired," and something, something. And I said. "I could..."

But he said, "You can't. You can't come in this room," and this and this.

But I said, "Maybe when Guru Dev is not here, when he is taking his bath, and I could clean or something."

And he said, "Yes, that time you can come but get out quickly, and don't disturb things." Like that. So I started on that, some cleaning of the floor, something, something, adjusting something.' Then one day, the pandit who dealt with ashram correspondence was away: One letter was there. It came for his blessing from some state in India asking that they are going to perform a big yagya and they want the blessings of Shankaracharya. And that letter was there and that date was approaching, about a week was left. And that I thought was a letter very responsible for the organisation to answer. And I asked Guru Dev, "Oh, oh, the answer of this letter?" And he would just not mind it, because in his eyes just one organisation doesn't mean anything, or something.

But, I thought it's a very great responsibility of the organisation, it's if, someone wants Shankaracharya's blessing then it's for the organisation to reply, and reply his blessings and create goodwill and inspire that organisation.' 'One day I said, "It's only about four, five days left. Shall I make a draft and read to Guru Dev, or anything?"

And He said, "What you will write?" And that was the end he said.'

Mahesh returned to his own room to gather his thoughts:

'I said, "Now come on, I have to write an answer to this. What? What? How to write? What to do? Now supposing if I was a Shankaracharya? What I'll say in that letter?" And I just imposed Shankaracharyaship on myself. And I said. "Yes, all the religious organisations look to Shankaracharya, head of the religion. The main thing is, that they should get inspiration from the blessing of Shankaracharya. As an organisation doing this great yagya, inspiring the people in the locality for religious life, so they should have the approval of Shankaracharya for this good act of religious value." I somehow wrote. And in the evening - it was just a very short thing, because nothing very long has to go from Shankaracharya, who is a great authority on religion, so very short inspiration. I made some few lines.

In the evening when I opened the door and entered and I read out that thing, in one simple breath quickly. And it sounded so apt, so appropriate. And then he said, "Will these people get it if you write? Then send it."

I said; "Yes, they can get it, it's yet four days." That's all he said. Then I quickly wrote and put on a seal of Shankaracharya and did the whole paraphernalia, and sent it. From that day probably I gave an impression that I could write something useful. That was the first thing. And from there, the letters came to me for replying and I was replying and sometimes reading to him.'

It is said that, in 1926, nineteen-year-old Hari Narayana Ojha became the disciple of Swami Brahmanand, and in 1931 the *guru* made him a *sannyasin*, naming him Swami Hariharananda, and that, in 1940, Swami Hariharananda approached Swami Brahmanand to ask him to become Shankaracharya.

'In the first instance, in 1948, Maharaj Shri wrote a note of inheritance to one of his best disciples, Swami Hariharananda Saraswati, but was famous by the name of Karpatri Ji. Their close associate, Brahmachari Yogeshwaranand, helped to write, and it was deposited there at Allahabad Registrar. But Swami Karpatri Ji's political motivations were greater, compared to his spiritual aspirations. Maharaj Shri had tried to convince him to take up the spiritual path to uplift the mankind. It was evident from the first that he was indifferent to his words. KarapatriJi said that he had decided to serve the nation through politics. Karpatri Ji persuades coolly and clearly, but Maharaj Shri now has to write another Will.' – extract from *'Hamare Gurudeva'*, Swami Vasudevanand Saraswati

In 1948 Swami Karpatri founds 'Akhil Bharatiya Ram Rajya Parishad', the 'All India Rama's Kingdom Assembly', a traditionalist Hindu political party. Swami Karpatri's protégé is a young man from Jabalpur, by the name of Pothiram Upadhyay, who is also heavily politicised having been, at the age of nineteen, a freedom fighter in the 'Quit India' civil disobedience campaign of 1942. Known as 'Revolutionary Sadhu'. Pothiram served prison sentences for his beliefs, one for cutting the telephone lines of the British government, and in all he served two terms, one of nine months at Varanasi prison and another of six months at Narsingpur prison. In Calcutta, on 31st December 1949, Revolutionary Sadhu is initiated as a *dandi sannyasi* by Shankaracharya Swami Brahmanand, and given the name Swami Swaroopanand Saraswati

Considering Swami Karpatri is viewed as the chief disciple of the Shankaracharya of Jyotirmath, and a traditionalist, he is unlikely to accept French singer, dancer and scholar, Alain Daniélou as his disciple. However, Daniélou (pictured left, standing with *sadhu*) claims Swami Karpatri is his teacher (of Shaivism) and that he has given him the name Shiva Sharan (Protected by Shiva).

Daniélou stays at Rewa Kothi, a mansion overlooking the Ganges at Varanasi, which he rents from the Maharajah of Rewa. There he immerses himself completely in Indian culture, translating Karpatri's writings, learning the veena, and producing recordings of local classical musicians.

A young truth-seeker writes to Swami Brahmanand in the hope of an audience:- *'Ramji went to meet Swamiji (Brahmananda) on the agreed date. It was twelve noon. In order to complete the afternoon rituals, Swamiji (Brahmananda) was on his way to get bath. Staring at Ramji once, Swamiji said, "Come on. We will bathe first".*

Ramji without a word followed him silently. At the end of the bath, Swamiji (Brahmananda) held his hand and said "Take an oath that you are into sannya now".

It was a shock for Ramji as there were to be a lot of preparations before the initiation ceremony. So he asked "Swamiji, do I need to recite the Gayatri mantra right now?"

Swamiji explained "I am not initiating you into sannyas now. But from now think yourself as you are sannyasi mentally. That is the first preparatory step that one should take".' – 'Hamare Gurudeva'

* * * * *

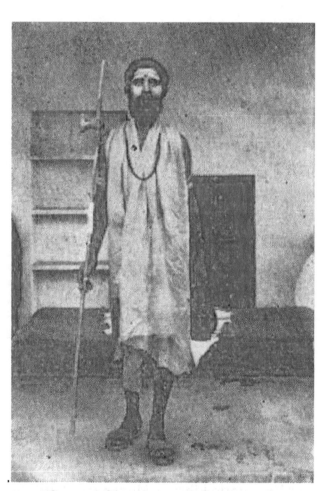

Swami Shantanand Saraswati

On 5th October 1951, Swami Brahmanand initiates Ramji Tripathi, one of his devotees, into *sannyas*, naming him Swami Shantanand Saraswati.

**Shankaracharya Swami Brahmanand Saraswati aboard mobile dais,
Old Square, near Mussoorie Library, Mussoorie, 23rd September 1952
note the steering wheel and front light of the vehicle**

'One should know as to how to live in the world and he will be happy. Your body and wealth is useful in the world and your mind is useful on the path to God. Do not apply too much mind in the world than necessary otherwise it would be a waste and a loss to both material and spiritual aspects of life. Just like putting more than necessary gum to paste the envelope. The gum will be wasted and the envelope will be spoiled'

- ashram publicity material 1942

'The world then is a dharmashala (a stopping house for pilgrims), four days you remain here, then you proceed further. Don't get very involved in any of the difficulties in your abode at the dharmashala, accomplish the work needed in order to go.'

'If having become a human being you do not obtain knowledge of Paramatma then understand that it is as if you have sold a diamond for the price of spinach.'

'Actually, Paramatma is like a "general merchant" in whose place there is no deficiency of any articles of happiness. But in order to gain his grace, regular effort is required, not only some reading of the greatness of Paramatma. By studying a catalogue, how can you become wealthy?'

- 'Shri Shankaracharya Upadeshamrit', '108 Discourses of Guru Dev'

Shankaracharya Swami Brahmanand Saraswati – New Delhi- November 1952

On 4th December 1952, in Delhi, President of India, Dr Rajendra Prasad met with Shankaracharya Swami Brahmananda Saraswati, for one and a half hours. Swami Brahmananda told him: -

"Before, the kings would have discussions with tapasviyon (ascetics) and maharshiyon (great saints) for their advice on the tasks of government. Because of yoga and tapasya (austerity) their minds had become clear. There existed neither greed nor worldly desires, and they did not fear the king becoming displeased with what they said. Those who were given advice, that advice was beneficial for both raja (king) and praja (subject). But now things have gone to hell on account of rajas neglecting to keep the company of maharshiyon.'

'What advice can your servant give you? Only that which your eyes will see. Therefore, you should wish to accept advice from maharshiyon who can also imagine the future. You people should not remain confused about this, opposing religious guidance and statecraft. Us folk giving upadesha (instruction) makes mankind righteous. However righteous mankind will be then, that much the government also proceeds with a very beautiful appearance.' – extract from *'Shri Jyotishpithoddharak', 'Biography of Guru Dev'*

**Shankaracharya Swami Brahmanand Saraswati
& President of India, Dr Rajendra Prasad, Delhi, 4th December 1952**

**President of India, Dr Rajendra Prasad standing with Brahmachari Mahesh
at 7 Canning Lane, New Delhi**

'*This historical incident was to be accomplished in 7 Canning Lane, New Delhi. Maharaj Shri sent for his two close servants, Rameshwar Prasad Tiwari and Shyam Narayan Gupta from Prayag, and Chowdary Krishnagopal, an advocate from Etawa, to accomplish the task mentioned above, for making the Will. Maharaj Shri chose his new "uttaradhikari" (successor) and wrote his name and whereabouts.*'

'*Maharaj Ji had Willed the entire peeth in the name of Swamiji, and named three other successors, with his signature, and witness signatures in front of advocate Chowdary. He had completed all the formalities, registered with the Registrar here in Allahabad and taken back the previous documents.*' – '*Hamare Gurudeva*'

Apparently, the *"Swamiji"* named in the Will asks his *guru* to reconsider, pointing out that he is but an insignificant *"shishya"* (disciple) amongst many excellent and qualified *shishya*, but the *guru* instructs him to accept.

He returns to his ashram in Varanasi, and, several months later, on Sunday 4th May Swami Brahmanand departs by the Delhi Mail train for Calcutta.

The *guru* stays at 86 Vali Ganj (Ballygunge) in Calcutta, where a doctor, said to be Shri Vidhan Chandra Roy, is in attendance. One night, the doctor checks him over and assures, '*sab thik hai*' ('All is well'). Ten minutes later the *guru* asks for assistance to get up, whereupon he sits crossed-legged and closes his eyes.

On Wednesday 20th May 1953, Shankaracharya Swami Brahmanand Saraswati breathes his last.

– 2 –

At the passing of the eighty-six year old *guru* his students are left in disarray. Brahmachari Satyanand recalls: -

'When in 1953 Guru Dev left this mortal frame and attained nirvana I was at Benares, another place of pilgrimage for Hindus, and at that moment I was staying in the ashram of Guru Dev. Everybody knew that I am very attached to Guru Dev and devoted to Guru Dev, and then news came to Benares that Guru Dev has attained nirvana. I was sitting somewhere with a group of my friends and the news was relayed there. When my friends heard that Guru Dev was no more they were very anxious about me and when they conveyed that news, they were rather alert to appraise whatever reaction is and what happened, I simply, when I heard that news I became very sad, very sorry and I just kept my head on the table before me. And all of them were very anxious what will become of me. But soon after, while I was very morose, sorrow, sad, entire world was empty for me and I did not understand what to do without Guru Dev, just a half a minute or two seconds after a flash came and it appeared to me that Guru Dev was scolding me;

"What a fool you are! You have been with me for all these many months and years, and you heard my discourses too. Is it a moment of feeling sorry? Why should you be sorry today? And you think that I am gone, where am I gone? Till now whenever you wanted to meet me you had to come to the place where I was, and today when I have attained nirvana, I am everywhere, I am omnipresent. Where have I gone? Very foolish for you to mourn on this occasion. I am with you, here, there, everywhere. Why should you be sorry?"

And the moment this flash came my face became very brilliant, I became very cheerful. And when I raised my head, my friends who were standing there very anxious and held in suspense, they were upset to see my brilliant and cheerful face. And then they said, "What has happened to you?" I said, "No you can't understand, nothing has happened to me, I am alright, now let me go back to the ashram and make the necessary arrangements".'

The following are a selection of excerpts from *'Hamare Gurudeva'* by Swami Vasudevanand, translated from the Hindi into English

'Swamiji (Swami Shantananda) was at that time on the banks of the Ganges. Staying in Karnavasa he was undertaking severe penance again. In between an evening bhajan session on the banks of the Ganges he happened to hear a news telecast of one of the

radio stations. Later, some devotees arrived at the hermitage of Swamiji to inform of the departure of Maharaj Shri. Swamiji left for Varanasi as soon as possible to participate in the funeral

'A meeting of all the devotees, disciples, religious leaders, saints, sages, scholars and prominent people was arranged in the leadership of Karpatri ji Maharaj. An interim committee was formulated which had the ability to take care of the entire peeth until the official formalities could be completed with the help of the Allahabad Registrar. As the name of the successor was not declared, the interim committee had the power to take all kinds of decisions including the wealth. The interim committee was supposed to hand over all the documents and power to the successor once the name was declared,

'The interim committee was presided over by Swami Swaroopananda Saraswati with the secretary as Pt Balakrishna Mishra who was also the secretary of Bharat Dharma Mahamandal. Other members were Pt Balakrishna Mishra, Kashipathi Tripathy of Varanasi, Yugul Kishore Tandan of Etawa, Jagadish Prasad Mishra of Jabalpur, Ganga Prasad Pandey of Prayag, Pt Dwarika Prasad Tripathy, Brahmachari Mahesh ji, Brahmachari Ramprasad ji and Shankaralal ji.

Some days after the death of the *guru*, a *vasiyat*, or Will, surfaces. According to the Will, the *guru* listed four potential candidates suitable to succeed him, who are, in order of suitability, Swami Shantanand Saraswati, Pandit Dwarika Prasad Tripati, (if he comes to accept *danda*, i.e. becomes a *sannyasi*), Swami Vishnudevanand Saraswati, and Swami Paramanand Saraswati MA. So, the *guru's* first choice of successor is Swami Shantanand.

The account from *'Hamare Gurudeva'* is again invaluable: -

'The interim committee gave the responsibility of bringing the documents related to the announcement of the successor to Ganga Prasad Lohiya, from the sub-registrar office which was situated near by Prayag [Allahabad].

'Here, Swami Shantananda Saraswati had left the place right after Maharaj Shri had passed away. Swamiji had reached Vrindavan and stayed for some time and came back to his favourite place Anupshahar of Varanasi. The documents were brought from the sub registrar office and put forth in the midst of the interim committee of prominent personalities. The president of the committee had issued an order to obey the instructions made by Maharaj Shri before he passed away. Hence Following the instructions, the committee had informed Swamiji (Shantananda). Swami Swaroopananda Saraswati had personally informed him about the intentions of Maharaj Shri.'

On 12th June 1953 the scene was set for the induction of Swami Shantanand Saraswati as the Abhinava Shankaracharya, the new Shankaracharya of Jyotir Math: -

'In charge of the ceremony was Swami Govindanand ji Maharaj who had left the place without informing anybody. He was in possession of the essential things for the ceremony. But the general secretary Pt Balakrishna Mishra with the help of other members such as Pandit Kashipathi Tripathy, Lohiya Pandey, Brahmachari Mahesh, Shankar Brahmachari, and Brahmachari Ramprasad tried hard to make all arrangements and invited all the dignitaries from across the nation. Representatives of all the religious centres, sannyasis, scholars, and spiritual leaders arrived at the pre-determined time and the ceremony began. With the blessings of saints and sages of the entire world, the ceremony was successfully completed.'

Shankaracharya Swami Shantanand Saraswati
Abhinava Shankaracharya, from 12th June 1953

'"Nirvanotsav", in the memory of Maharaj Shri Swami Brahmananda Saraswati, and the scholar's meeting, which is widely known as Pandita Sabhaa, were arranged as part of the main ceremony. The entire program was organized in such a way that even today the devotees remember it as one of its kind.

'After the program had completed successfully, Swamiji on the seventh day had left for Prayag [Allahabad]. Interim committee had handed over the charge of the entire peeth to Swamiji. Swamiji in the light of way of management of his predecessors started serving the mankind and guiding the aspirants in the path of Spirituality.

'It is a well-known tradition that there will be three aspirants selected for the holy seat of the peeth and one among them will be finally chosen who will deserve the place in all dimensions. It will aid in choosing the best character for the holy seat of guiding thousands of followers. Hence there will always be a possibility of dissatisfaction among others and their followers for not choosing them. The same had taken place here too. A few unhappy people wanted to discard the ceremony and appoint somebody else to the holy position. But Pt Satyanarayan Kaviraj and chief of the management Pt Raj Narayan Shukla stopped all their efforts and stood like pillars in the support of ongoing ceremony. Yet they have established the support of Dwarika Prasad Shastri for their proposed task.

'A few self-declared scholars too were unhappy and stretched their helping hand in order to gain personal benefits. They also tried to make Swami Krishna Bodhashram Ji Maharaj as the Shankaracharya of the Jyothishpeeth. He was a tyaagi, a humble, simple and scholarly saint who had no selfish agenda to accomplish.'

On 23rd June 1953 Karpatri challenges the Will ot his *guru* and appoints his choice of *swami* as Shankaracharya, someone who is not one of Swami Brahmanand's disciples.

There are now two claimants to the title of Shankaracharya of Jyotir Math, Swami Shantanand Saraswati and Swami Krishnabodhashram.

Shri Shankaracharya Upadesha - Discourse of Shri Shankaracharya

The next issue of the *ashram* newsletter, *'Shri Shankaracharya Upadesha'*, is published on 20th July 1953, and contains a lengthy piece on the topic of the *guru's* Will under the title 'The Last Instruction of Anantashri Vibhushit Jyotishpith Adhishwara Jagadguru Shankaracharya Brahmibhut Swami Brahmanand Saraswati'.

Here is an extract from the three and a quarter page article, translated from the Hindi: -

"In connection with the vasiyat (Will), there have been erroneous false words printed in the newspapers. The correct news is this, that in the vasiyat are many pages of type, and Maharaj Shri signed on each and every page, and at the end is the signature of eyewitnesses. The vasiyat had been inserted in a heavy envelope and enveloped in cloth, was stitched and all were enclosed in another envelope, and on that were attached seals. The hypotheses that the signatures of Maharaj Shri were obtained without his knowledge, or in a condition when he did not have the strength to notice are completely baseless. The process of producing the vasiyat is dependent on the rule of the Registrar, according to which it had been produced.

According to the determination of the aforesaid Interim Committee, on 12th June 1953, in Brahmanivas Ashram, completed as prescribed by the Scriptures, was the abhishek (installation) of Shri Swami Shantanand Saraswati Ji. Wise dandi sannyasis, town leaders, and a collection of disciples were in attendance. And according to the vasiyat, he is the Jagatguru Shankaracharya of Jyotish Peeth. Also, by them is the management of the Peeth functioning.

Some people making erroneous publicity in connection with the vasiyat, they are writing untrue words in the newspapers, whose proper response is right here in the vasiyat in anka (issue number) 50, varsh (year) 3, of 'Shri Shankaracharya Upadesha' (the ashram's newsheet). After the great shock of reading this, if he has any doubts those good selves can look to redress from the mantri (chairman) of the Prayag circle of disciples. Here, for the circle of disciples, in the vasiyat is given all instructions, from which all disciples fulfil the desires of Brahmibhut Jagadguru, and they understand what is proper for them to do. In his own vasiyat, Maharaj wrote: -

"Before today I wrote a closed vasiyat on 23-10-43 (23rd October 1943) and placed it securely with the Registrar gentleman in Prayag. Now, by way of this present vasiyat I refute and cancel the above-mentioned vasiyat. This new vasiyat, if I shall not get cancelled or exchanged in my own life, this then will signify my last vasiyat, and accordingly, afterwards according to this vasiyat will the management be done of Shri Jyotish Peeth and Shri Swami Krishnanand Saraswati ashram and the connected pathshala (school), Brahma Vidya Niketan and the mandir (temple) of Brahmanadeshwar Mahadeva.

Therefore, together with earnest good consideration, without being influenced by opportune wilfulness or anything else, by way of writing my own vasiyat in this form, the parampara (succession) of Shri Jyotish Peeth acharya with stay uninterrupted, sanatana dharma (eternal dharma – i.e. Hinduism) and supporter of varna, the standing rule of Jyotish Peeth and clear aim of detailed instructions of the institution pertaining to Jyotish Peeth, the appointment of their own successor as Shankaracharya, and their duties, I am writing a detailed description of the suitable authority, also that settled to my own holy remembered gurudeva, the Shri 108 Swami Krishnanand Saraswati Trust, and the settlement and burden of arrangements of all the connected property, and by this vasiyat is consigned my own successor the parampara of Jyotish Peeth Adhishwar, by means of this above-mentioned vasiyat, management and adjustment, the first vasiyats having been terminated, this vasiyat is proved by my own signature, this is my very last vasiyat and it is really the chief obligation that I will protect my disciples.

Paush Shukla 2 Guruvar san. 2006, accordingly, 18th December 52
Brahmanand

* * * * *

It is recorded that in 1953, Swami Shantanand Saraswati files an official application claiming succession of Jyotir Math - case No. 44, of 1953 - registered with the Court Civil Judge, Allahabad.

Shri 108 Shri Swami Ji Krishnanand Saraswati
guru of Swami Brahmanand Saraswati

– 3 –

Not long after the ceremony making Swami Shantanand the Shankaracharya, Brahmachari Mahesh, the *ashram* secretary for over a decade, leaves Varanasi and heads off for Uttar Kashi, in the far north of India.

Brahmachari Mahesh's destination in Uttarkashi is an *ashram* called Gyan Mandir, the 'Temple of Knowledge Ashram' that likely once belonged to Swami Krishnanand, Swami Brahmanand's *guru*, whom he had met at Uttar Kashi when he was but a child. Leaving his comfortable home and parents at nine-years old, he heard his mother say; *'But don't become a bhikhamangaa* (beggar) *sadhu and when you get the desire sometime, for being a grishastha* (householder) *then come home at once.'* But instead he became a *sannyasi*, and in time, and after much persuasion, he accepted the post of Shankaracharya of Jyotir Math, the most powerful office of *sanatana dharma*, Hinduism.

Far from the commotion caused by the succession dispute, Mahesh finds rest in this tranquil valley of the Himalayan foothills:

'Where I stay in a small Ashram in Uttar Kashi, the cave is like a small basement under a room. The entrance is through an opening only big enough for one person to enter.'

'Food is not always needed, but when I am eating, a man comes from the village and cooks vegetables. I do not break silence by seeing or talking to anyone.'

- *'Hermit in the House'*, Helena Olson

* * * * *

Apparently, in January 1954, at the Munsiff Court in Lucknow, followers of Swami Krishnabodhaashram apply for an injunction against Swami Shantanand, restraining him from interfering with any of the Jyotir Math properties. It is also recorded that another suit is filed with the Court of District Judge, this one in Varanasi, brought by Swami Paramanand Saraswati and three others, versus someone referred to as Ram Ji Tripathi - Swami Shantanand Saraswati's name before he became a *sannyasi*.

* * * * *

Rumour has it, that when an aunt of Mahesh became ill, he was asked to accompany her to a health facility in Madanapalle in south India. Anyway, he leaves Uttarkashi and settles in Madanapalle instead. Eventually, the *brahmachari* decides to continue his travels, moving further south to visit temples in Kanchi, Rameshwaram and Kanya Kumari. Whilst touring he lectures and teaches a form of meditation.

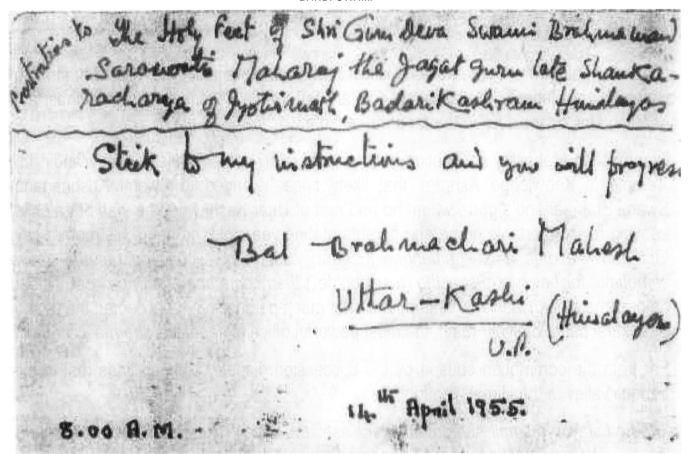

'Stick to my instructions and you will progress' - 14th April 1955
Bal Brahmachari Mahesh

The system of meditation Mahesh Ji teaches gains increasing popularity, and in October 1955 a conference is convened in Kerala, ostensibly to celebrate the life of Shankaracharya Swami Brahmanand Saraswati. Invitations are sent far and wide, even to senior members of Government The initiative wins the approval of Swami Shantanand, who sends his letter of support in Sanskrit, and dictates a note in English in which he says; 'I hope your efforts will promote the development of spirituality, nobility, calmness and bliss. Remember the teaching and ideal of Shrimad Bhagavad Gita.' Here Shantanand quotes the Bhagavad Gita, Chapter 9, verse 27: -

यत्करोषि यदश्नासि यज्जुहोषि ददासै यत्।

यत्तपस्यसि कौन्तेय तत्कुरुष्व मदर्पणम॥

'Whatever action you do, whatever you eat,
whatever you offer in sacrifice, whatever you give,
Whatever austerities you perform, O Kaunteya (Arjuna), do that as an offering unto Me.'

[Messages]

Your Efforts will Promote Spirituality Nobility Calmness & Bliss

Blessings of
SHRI BHAGWAN SHANKARACHARYA, JYOTIRMATH
Badarikashram, Himalayas.

❋ श्री: ❋

श्रीमत्परमहंसपरिव्राजकाचार्य्यपदवाक्यप्रमाणपारावारापरीणयमनियमासनप्राणायामप्रत्याहारधा-रणाध्यानसमा व्यष्टाङ्गयोगानुष्ठाननिष्ठतपश्चर्य्याचरणचक्रवर्त्यनादिगुरुपरम्पराप्राप्तवैदिकदर्शनमतस्थापनाचा-र्य्यसकलनिगमागमसारहृदयवैदिकमार्गप्रवर्तकसर्वतन्त्रस्वतन्त्रचातुर्वर्ग्यशिक्षकश्रीमन्महाराजाधिराजगुरुभूमण्ड-लाचार्य्यजगद्गुर्वनन्तश्रीविभूषितश्रीमदादिशङ्कराचार्य्यभगवत्पादपद्मभृङ्गायमानाः श्रीमदनेकशासनतिरस्कृता-न्तेवासिजनमनस्तमस्तोमाः शश्वत्सार्वभौमविश्वजनीनसनातनधर्मसंरक्षणबद्धपरिकराः परापरविद्याविद्योतितान्तः-करणः समस्तसम्प्रदायसमन्वयसाधन दत्तचित्ता विविधविरुदावलिविराजमानमानोन्नता अलक्नन्दागङ्गातीर-निवस्युत्तराम्नायश्रीमज्जयोतिष्पीठाधीश्वराः श्रीमद्शान्तानन्दसरतीस्वामिवर्य्या विजयन्तेतराम् ।

Brahma Niwas, Alopibag.
Allahabad, U. P., 20—10—'55.

Beloved devotees,

I am in receipt of your kind letter addressed to His Holiness Jagadguru Bhagwan Shri Sankaracharya Anant Shri Vibhushit Swami Shantananda Saraswathi Ji Maharaj, Jyotirmath, Badarikashram. His Holiness has very kindly directed me to express His Feeling of pleasure, to all of you for organising a spiritual Development conference at Cochin from 23rd instant, under the auspices of Shri Shankaracharya Brahmanand Saraswathi Adhyatmic Vikas Mandal of Kerala, His Holiness wishes to convey the following message.

"Spirituality is the backbone of India. India can restore her ancient glory only through Religion and Spirituality. All religion is simply an attempt to unveil the essential nature of own-selves. This ultimate Truth can be realised through self-purification. I hope your efforts will promote the development of spirituality, nobility, calmness and bliss. Remember the teaching and the ideal of Shrimad Bhagwat Gita:—

यत्करोषि यदश्नासि यज्जुहोषि ददासि यत् ।
यत्तपस्यसि कौन्तेय तत्कुरुष्व मदर्पणम् ॥

I am extremely pleased to know that Bal Brahmachari Mahesh Yogi, the beloved disciple of Guru Deva, Brahmaleen Mahayogiraj Jagadguru Bhagwan Shri Shankaracharya Anant Shri Vibhushit Swami Brahmananda Saraswathi Ji Maharaj of Jyothirmath Badarikashram is helping the cause of spirituality there. May his presence in Kerala inspire you all with **Real Peace and Happiness.**

"I wish your Maha Sammelan every success"

With love and blessings of

Gurudev Jai Ram Misra.

S/d-

Secretary,

His Holiness Jagatguru Bhagwan Shri Shankaracharya Anant Sri Vibhushit Swami Shantanand Saraswathi Ji Maharaj, Jyotirmath Badarikashram.

BEACON LIGHT OF THE HIMALAYAS

ADHYATMIC VIKAS MANDAL

FLAG HOISTING

THE DAWN OF A HAPPY NEW ERA

IN THE FIELD OF SPIRITUAL PRACTICES

MIND CONTROL, PEACE

&

ATMANANDA

Through simple & easy methods of Spiritual Sadhana

propounded

by

Maharshi Bala Brahmachari Mahesh Yogi Maharaj

OF

UTTAR KASI, HIMALAYAS.

SOUVENIR OF THE GREAT SPIRITUAL DEVELOPMENT CONFERENCE OF KERALA., OCTOBER, 1955.

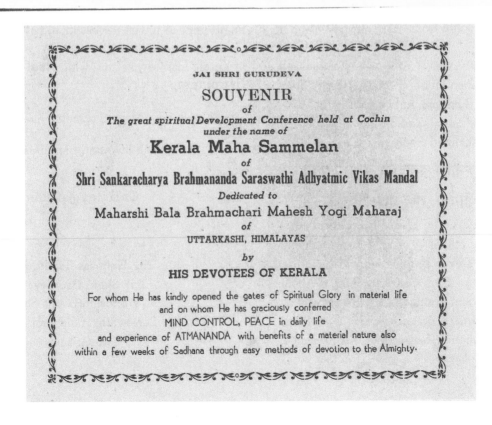

JAI SHRI GURUDEVA

SOUVENIR

of

*The great spiritual Development Conference held at Cochin
under the name of*

Kerala Maha Sammelan

of

Shri Sankaracharya Brahmananda Saraswathi Adhyatmic Vikas Mandal

Dedicated to

Maharshi Bala Brahmachari Mahesh Yogi Maharaj

of

UTTARKASHI, HIMALAYAS

by

HIS DEVOTEES OF KERALA

For whom He has kindly opened the gates of Spiritual Glory in material life
and on whom He has graciously conferred
MIND CONTROL, PEACE in daily life
and experience of ATMANANDA with benefits of a material nature also
within a few weeks of Sadhana through easy methods of devotion to the Almighty.

OUR SPIRITUAL GUIDE

His Holiness Maharshi
Bala Brahmachari
Mahesh Yogi Maharaj.
Uttarkasi, Himalayas.

Oh ye of the peaceless and suffering humanity!

My happiness desires to root out your suffering. Will you extend your arm and allow me to lift you up from the mire of misery and peacelessness?

Come on, here is the call of peace and joy for you. Here is an invitation, a cordial invitation for you all to come and enjoy the Blissful Grace and All Powerful Blessings of my Lord the Great Swami Brahmanand Saraswati, the Great among the greats of the Himalayas. I have found a treasure in the Dust of His Lotus Feet and now I invite you to share it with me and make yourself happy.

Come on; I invite you to get into the Blissful Realm of His Universal Benevolence. See, the path is straight and entry is free. Come on with faith and you will find that the very cause of your peacelessness and misery will be eradicated and you will be adorned with lasting peace and real happiness in your day to day life.

Feel not disappointment in life and shirk not from your responsibilities in despair. Whatever are your circumstances, rich or poor, if you are not in peace and if you want peace and happiness, come on with faith and you will have it. Here is the message of hope for you. Here is the Divine Call of rescue for you. Peace and joy of living await you. Do not reject it. Come on and have it.

The sun of Guru Deva's Blessings is now up on the horizon. Wake up from the deep slumber of apathy and agony and enjoy all glories of life material and divine.

Bal Brahmachari Mahesh.
28.11.55

35

The souvenir booklet, published as 'The Beacon Light of the Himalayas', contains a handwritten message from 'Bal Brahmachari Mahsh', many photographs, letters of support, guest speeches and the transcripts of several lectures. Within the pages of the booklet, Brahmachari Mahesh is repeatedly referred to by the highly respectful title of 'Maharshi' or 'Great Seer'.

* * * * *

1955 sees the release of *'Anthologie de la musique classique de l'Inde'*; a collection of recordings made by Alain Daniélou for the International Music Council. The anthology of music features several Indian classical musicians, including Ravi Shankar and Ali Akhbar Khan, neither of whom has had a record released in the west.

* * * * *

When, in the spring of 1958, Maharishi announces his wish to travel overseas in order to spread the message of meditation, arrangements are soon made for him to do so. On 27th April 1958 he checks onto a plane at Calcutta Airport, on a flight to Burma. After a stay in Rangoon he continues on his way, visiting Thailand, Malaya, Singapore, Hong Kong and Hawaii, before eventually arriving in the United States of America.

By May 1959 Maharishi is lecturing and teaching meditation at the Masquers Club, an actors' club in Hollywood. He is soon joined by a few of his fellow countrymen, Ram Rao, and brother and sister Lakshmana & 'Mata Ji', who are from a very wealthy family in Calcutta, and excursions are organised to sightsee around Los Angeles and Disneyland.

From America Maharishi heads off to Europe where, he gets established there too with many people attracted to his teachings, and many 'initiated' into meditation.

Maharishi explains how bliss is the nature of reality, and cites a verse that explains this - Taittiriya Upanishad 3:6: -

आनन्दाध्येव खल्विमानि भूतानि जायन्ते।

आनन्देन जातानि जीवन्ति।

आनन्दं प्रयन्त्यभिसंविशन्तीति।

सैषा भार्गवी वारुणी विद्या।

परमे व्योमन्प्रतिष्ठिता।

'There is a whole thing about…

"aanandaadhyeva khalvimaani bhuutaani jaayante." - "From ananda alone all these beings are born"

"aanandena jaataani jiivanti." - "In the ananda" - ananda is bliss, ocean of happiness. "In ananda they live."

"aanandam prayantyabhisanvishantiiti." - "Unto ananda they dissolve, at the time of dissolution."

He has various well wishers in London, two of whom are particularly well-placed, Leon McLaren and Dr Francis Roles, the men behind the London School of Economic Science and the Study Society, who arrange for Maharishi to speak at the Royal Albert Hall on 13th March 1961.

As his mission expands, Maharishi readily acknowledges the need to train teachers, or 'initiators' as they are known, in order to spread this system of meditation more rapidly. Therefore, plans to build an academy in India are formulated so that 'Spiritual Guides Courses' can be arranged for training meditation teachers. Soon construction is started on Dhyan Vidhya Peeth, the Academy of Meditation, at a 14-acre site on the edge of the jungle in the foothills of the Himalayas, next to the River Ganges, at Rishikesh, on land leased by the Forestry Department.

The first of Maharishi's teacher training courses, in Rishikesh, India, is blessed by Shankaracharya Swami Shantanand Saraswati, who visits the course on Tuesday 30th May 1961 and tells the assembled students: -

'Rishikesh is a place where so many saints and sages meditated with a view to attaining Self-realisation. Every grain of sand is vibrating forth the holy influence of saints and sages who have inhabited this part of India since ages past.'

His Holiness Shantanand Saraswati commends Maharishi's method of meditation, describing it as a: - *'master key to the knowledge of Vedanta'*, and adds, *'There are other keys, but a master key is enough to open all the locks.'*

One of the course participants, who are learning how to teach meditation, is Doctor Roles, a follower of P. D. Ouspensky (himself a disciple of the notable G. I. Gurdjieff). In meeting with the Shankaracharya, Dr Roles soon realises he has found the spiritual advisor he seeks for his London-based Study Society, and for the London School of Economic Science, run by Leon McLaren and himself. Much to Maharishi's annoyance, the two men then go on to form a breakaway organisation, The School of Meditation, in London.

In 1965, when Leon MacLaren first has an audience with HH Shrî Shântânanda Saraswatî, His Holiness starts the series of audiences and conversations, which would go on until 1993, saying:

'It is not my desire which has to be carried out. The desire which has to be helped, is that which arises in people looking for the truth, wishing to acquire the divine life and to make efforts in that direction; and so far as I can, I will always be ready. My door is always open to anyone, known or unknown, eastern or western, irrespective of his upbringing or culture, because in fact we all come from the same stock. As long as that desire and the decision are strong, permanent and stable, the help will always be available.

With the first impulse of creation, the system is embodied in the Vedas. All knowledge is embodied in them. With the help of the Vedas and the Shâstras (holy scriptures) people can lead a natural life. But in this great drama due to multifarious movements in the creation when people are in illusion and forget the real part, taking themselves to be true, then it becomes necessary that some direction be given to them, so that they can understand their part which has to be played, and played nicely.'

photo: Frank Papentin

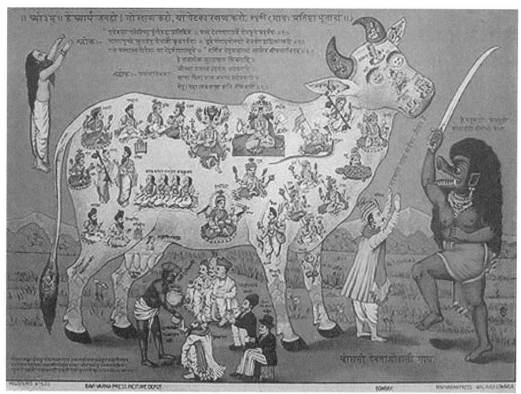

chaurasi devataovali gaaya - The Cow with 84 Deities
Ravi Varma Press, c1912

यद्‌गृहे दुःखिता गावः स याति नरके नरः।

"yadgrihe duhkhitaa gaavah sa yaati narake narah."
'The man who gives suffering to the cow goes to hell.'

"Schemes to slaughter and kill are the downfall of the cow and its progeny, and injure the holy and financial delights of both raja and subject. So for this reason everyone should make an effort to put a stop to these gristly practices. Several states have done laudable work in this connection, but unless central government will be compelled, it is impossible to satisfactorily inform of the effects. For the sake of this, effort should be made countrywide."

- Swami Brahmanand Saraswati, Shankaracharya of Jyotirmath 1941-1953
quoted in 1946 *'Godhana'* issue of *'Kalayana'* (Gita Press, Gorakhpur)

Gau-Raksha, the ban of cow slaughter, is a long-standing demand of India, endorsed by Mahatma Gandhi. But, on the 7th of November 1966, whilst Jawaharlal Nehru's daughter, Shrimati Indira Gandhi, is Prime Minister of India, a hundred thousand holy people, who are demanding a ban on cow slaughter, march on parliament and several saints are shot. A cow is killed also, and Swami Karpatri is whipped and cruelly treated. Allegedly, the death of the cow prompts Karpatri to predict the demise of Indira Gandhi and her family.

* * * * *

The Beatles in India with Maharishi Mahesh Yogi - 1968
photo Paul Saltzman, All Rights Reserved.

– 4 –

News that Maharishi's next public lecture will be his last public appearance is enough to persuade John Lennon, George Harrison, Paul McCartney and Ringo Starr of The Beatles to buy tickets to attend. After the lecture, given at the London Hilton in September 1967, The Beatles are given a private audience with Maharishi after which they learn Transcendental Meditation (TM). The Beatles and their partners join Maharishi's meditation course in Bangor, Wales, which is also attended by the singer of The Rolling Stones, Mick Jagger with his girlfriend, Marianne Faithfull.

The Beatles - John Lennon and George Harrison in particular - become staunch advocates of Transcendental Meditation, and appear on the popular David Frost show, screened on British television. The Beatles record *'Across the Universe'*, with a refrain that includes an indirect reference to Maharishi, *'Nothing's going to change our world, Jai Guru Deva'* - *'Jai Guru Deva'* is *'Victory to Guru Dev'*, and refers to Maharishi's master.

Early in 1968, The Beatles and their companions are set to join Maharishi on his next course in India, scheduled for the spring. The 1968 Spiritual Guides Course is attended by dozens of participants from across the world, including The Beatles and other celebrities, such as Mike Love of the Beach Boys, folk singer Donovan, actress Mia Farrow and her sister Prudence Farrow (of 'Dear Prudence' fame). Whilst on the course The Beatles write many of the songs that will appear on their next record, the double album entitled 'The Beatles', better known as 'The White Album'. One tune that doesn't make it onto the The Beatles record is a ditty, one of many they make up in India, which goes something like this: -

I'd like to thank you Guru Dev
Just for being Our Guiding Light - Guru Dev, Guru Dev, Guru Dev
I'd like to thank you Guru Dev
Just for Seeing us through the night - Guru Dev, Guru Dev, Guru Dev
The Spiritual Regeneration World-wide Found-ation

A - B - C - D - E - F - G - H - I - Jai Guru Dev
A - B - C - D - E - F - G - H - I - Jai Guru Dev

We'd like to thank you Guru Dev
Cos your children couldn't thank you enough - Guru Dev, Guru Dev, Guru Dev
We'd like to thank you Guru Dev
Cos your children couldn't thank you enough - Guru Dev, Guru Dev, Guru Dev
The Spiritual Regeneration World-wide Found-ation – Of India!

VIA RISHIKESH

In 1970, a young couple, Englishman Paul Mason and his Italian girlfriend Yolanda Baldi, succeed in a rather ambitious plan to hitchhike their way from Great Britain to North Africa, through the Middle East and then to India, on very little money. Whilst in India they decide to visit the Maharishi's *ashram* - it seems only natural, given the coverage the world's press had given to The Beatles' visit.

The *ashram* is open to visitors though overnight accommodation is not on offer, despite the fact that the place is virtually uninhabited. Living at the *ashram* are some of Maharishi's *brahmacharis* (monks) and a few Europeans who perform various support functions there, such as running the Heidelberg printing press and teaching meditation to visitors, whilst they await the Maharishi's return. The hitchhikers stay at another *ashram*, but make daily visits to Maharishi's *ashram* to learn more about meditation. Their month's visit to Rishikesh is included as part of an account of their travels, published as; *'Via Rishikesh: A Hitchhiker's Tale'*.

* * * * *

From 1971 onwards, Maharishi decides to hold his international teacher training courses elsewhere, in USA, in Spain and in Switzerland, so his *ashram* then becomes used solely by Indians, with all operations under the watchful eye of Brahmachari 'Swami' Satyanand. The *ashram* swiftly expands, with multi-storey buildings being erected to cater for the influx of ever-greater numbers of participants, with separate quarters designated specifically for women.

Adjacent to Maharishi's 'bungalow' (the three-storey house where Maharishi stays when he is on site) are built the numerous *kutirs* known as 'Chaurasia Kutir', domed meditation rooms intended for long-term stay visitors. The word *'chaurasia'* is a Sanskrit word meaning 'eighty-four', sometimes used to refer to a specific group of supernatural deities. Whether or not there were ever actually as many as eighty-four *kutirs* planned for Dhyan Vidhya Peeth is doubtful.

Shankaracharya Swami Shantanand Saraswati & his close supporters

In February 1973, S. M. Jaiswal translates a speech by His Holiness Shrî Shântânanda Sarasvatî, in which he says: *'The difficulty of transmission through different languages certainly creates a formidable barrier. Even so, whatever has been passed on to you is fairly useful. In the course of these deliberations, it is obvious that knowledge, even as a piece of information, is the initial thing; for it is only knowledge that initiates activity. If one does not know about a beautiful place, one would never have a desire to go to see the place. So one must acquire the knowledge first. The information aspect of knowledge is only the outer or physical aspect. The deeper aspects appear only when the information is put into practice. This is known as 'anubhava', experience of the knowledge arising from the interaction of the individual (vyashti) and the universal (samashti) under the light of that particular knowledge or information. Only here does the real test of the validity of the knowledge and the sincerity of the individual materialise. Unless the knowledge has been brought into the workings of all three bodies of the individual, the particular knowledge does not become universal and, having fulfilled its purpose of information, returns into useless matter. One can see this from the examples of so-called learned people, who can speak on their subject, or any subject, at any time, but their life is not governed by their knowledge, which remains barren to produce peace and bliss, either for them of for their people and students. So much use is made of the word these days, but nothing seems to mean anything. The meaning is in the action; action is the interaction of the individual (vyashti) and the universal (samashti). In this interaction is the universal or the meaning of the word. To realise the word is to find its universal, which is harder than speaking or writing. Not having realised the meaning, people start giving meanings to words and, so as no one wants to lag behind, so you have many more unrealisable meanings to a word. This is nothing but confusion. When you and your people put these words into action, the cloud of confusion will be dissolved, the real meaning will shine through and understanding will descend. Meanwhile, you will have to face situations of confusion and conflicts. Word and meanings may not be clear, but one does not have to worry about it. The practice of the knowledge given would clear the way and the vision. No one needs to bind himself to a word; one does need to transcend it. To transcend a word is to put the word in action, after which it shines with more brilliance. One must keep on transcending till the word once again becomes fully charged with full truth, consciousness and bliss. With this message you should go back to your people and to your land and from your personal practice and experience, you should guide them with knowledge and practice of knowledge and thus enrich the society and nation. Blessings for all.'*

* * * * *

Since the death of Swami Brahmanand in 1953, Swami Swaroopanand studies under other teachers, such as Krishna Bodha Asrama, and Abhinava Sacchidananda Tirtha of Dwaraka.

Swami Krishna Bodhashram

On 10th September 1973 Swami Krishna Bodha Ashram dies and Swami Swaroopananda Saraswati is named as his successor, as Shankaracharya of Jyotirmath. Swami Karpatri sits by him during his investiture.

* * * * *

In the late 1960's and early 1970's several Indian spiritual teachers arrived in the west to spread their teachings and techniques. One such teacher is Acharya Rajneesh, who hails from Jabalpur, is known to his followers as 'Bhagwan', and has spawned a multitude of adoring fans known as the 'Orange People'. Curiously, Rajneesh is happy to tell disparaging stories about fellow teachers - his tales are his stock-in-trade: -

'You will be surprised to know that in the twentieth century, one of the Hindu leaders - the most respected Hindu leader, Swami Karpatri was teaching. I was present in the meeting, and I had to contradict him and I created thousands of enemies because of that. A new dam was being got ready just a few miles away, and this place was going to be the most benefited because of the dam, because their lands were dry and the rains were not certain, and they would be getting as much water as they wanted. And what the man was saying to them was, "Don't accept that water, because before giving you the water they take the electricity out of it."

Now, to the people he was saying that that water is impotent; its whole potential has been taken out. "It is dangerous for you to take that water- refuse." And the people looked convinced, because without education they don't understand that electricity is not something you take out of the water, it is not something like sexual potentiality that you can take out of a man and he becomes impotent. But this simile convinced them, and they were raising their hands in support.'

'One of the great Hindu monks, Karpatri, has written a whole book against me; and when I saw it I wondered how he managed. Statements that I have never made he makes in my name, and then criticizes them. Now, anybody reading his book will think that he has finished me completely. He has not even touched me.'

This is possibly a reference to a book of Rajneesh's entitled, *'From Sex to Superconsciousness'* to which Swami Karpatri asks *'Kya Sambhog se Samadhi?'* *'What, Samadhi From Sex?'*

It is difficult to research the works of Swami Karpatri as he does not speak or write in English, only in Hindi and Sanskrit. This is also the situation with regards Swami Swaroopanand too.

* * * * *

In February 1974 His Holiness Shrî Shântânanda Sarasvatî says: *'The present age is full of disruptive forces and everywhere turmoil is being experienced. So it is very necessary that some good work to rescue humanity and to relieve the trouble should be provided; so that if and when they turn towards this work, they should also be able to experience peace and bliss and beautify and enlarge their life. Through the ages a number of systems have been given. Some are hard compared with others; some are long in relation to time. The system of meditation which has been given to us is the culmination of all simplicity by which the evolution of mankind is most easy. The Vedas and the scriptures have been given but have become far removed from the common life of today and now seem hard to practice and follow. This seemingly can be eliminated by the proper practice of meditation. The information which one receives from different philosophical systems are there and if one took to meditation properly, one would see that the experiences of all the truth and bliss is available and one would not be expected to go through those hard disciplines of which this age is not very capable. Let the main emphasis be placed on meditation, which alone will help all of us on the causal level. Then we could help society, which needs our help. Blessings be with you. '*

In the winter of 1978, hitchhiker Paul Mason buys a plane ticket and returns to India to further explore: -.

'I journey for several days up atrocious, dangerous mountain roads, in order to visit Joshimath, high in mountains. Eventually, I arrive at the distant market town of Joshimath, high up in the stony regions. The nights are amazing there, the stars are so very clear and visible amongst the snowy peaks of the surrounding mountains, it is as if you can just reach out and touch the points of bright light. I imagine to myself that this is where astrology must have first been studied.

The area around the simple town of Joshimath is peaceful other than when the Indian soldiers patrolling the border with China decide to have some rifle practice.

I find a warm welcome at Swami Shantanand's Jyotir Math *ashram*, and wander around the neat buildings and the tidy gardens. Inside, I drink in the atmosphere and admire the paintings of Lord Shiva, Adi Shankara, and Swami Brahmanand Saraswati.

An aged monk shows me a selection of publications, two of which appear to be on the life and teachings of Swami Brahmanand Saraswati. They are both in Hindi, but I make a pact with myself, to learn enough Hindi and Sanskrit in order to translate them one day, and get them published.

Nearby to the little monastery of Jyotir Math, a walk of a few minutes is the ancient mulberry tree, said to be two thousand years old! The tree stands very near to the venerated cave of Adi Shankara, the founder of the Shankaracharya order of monks.

On the path back to town I discover the Trotakacharya Gupha, the cave of the foremost disciple of the legendary Adi Shankara, the man who, centuries ago, established the Shankaracharya maths in the four corners of India. I sit to meditate there, and am there but a few minutes before being interrupted. It is a young Indian clad in white, who appears ill at ease. He indicates I should leave at once. I wonder what his reaction would have been had we shared the same colour skin.

On making enquiries, I later find the cave has been purchased for use as an *ashram*, and it is rumoured in the marketplace that Swami Swaroopanand has financial backing in Benares (Varanasi).'

'On 25th December 1978, Christmas Day, I journey to Uttar Kashi. Once there, with pack on back, I make my way out of town, and trudge on and on. The shadows stretch ever longer and the light is fading quite dramatically before I eventually arrive at the quaint little *ashram*. I read the notice, the *ashram* is called 'Gyan Mandir', and I am drawn to the stone Shivalinga that stands at the entrance there.

The *swamis* at the *ashram* welcome me, and a few of them chatter to me attentively, but there seems to be embarrassment that they cannot provide anything more than very basic accommodation. "No proper facilities!" they explain. Nonetheless, they offer me to stay in a quaint and very primitive room, which I accept. I am befriended by one of them in particular, an old *swami* called Swami Ashibananda, and feel assured that I will be happy here.

Entrance of Gyan Mandir *ashram*, Gyan Su, near Uttar Kashi

Once inside the little room, with its hard mud floor, I lit a candle and a stick of *agarbatti,* roll out my sleeping bag on the raised bed to sit on, and settle down to meditate, and then turn in.

During the night it gets very cold, so I am so-o-o glad that I have taken a friend's advice and brought along a 'space-blanket' which I wrap tightly around myself. Perhaps it was the journey from Srinagar, Garhwal or maybe I ate too much glacé pineapple but I do feel ill. In fact, I get incredibly feverish and feel inspired to wrap myself in an emergency space-blanket - I really start to cook inside, which is actually far more preferable than freezing without it! But, the fever makes me so sick, and I have to get up and go outside. I then scurry back and get snug and safe back inside my space-blanket again. There I fall into this incredible ecstatic state, colourful and incredibly blissful, like a trance. Pretty much a relief from all the ill stuff!

In the morning I go outside to the standing tap to freshen up and clean my teeth, and there I find a brahmachari washing there. We exchange nods and smiles etc, and I get on with cleaning my teeth. Then he asks me where I am staying - so I point weakly to the door of my room. He looks at me curiously and then says very slowly: - "Ah - that is where Mahesh Yogi stayed."

'Well, when I return to my room I look about more closely. I notice a gap on the front side of the bed and find that if I remove some sticks I can crawl underneath and into a small space below ground level. Seems to be the *gupha*, the 'cave' Maharishi describes to Helena Olson in 'Hermit in the House'. I don't explore immediately but when I do I clamber through the narrow gap and enter the space beneath, which is somewhat claustrophobic. I can hear a faint but persistent hissing sound, probably on account of the River Bhagirathi (Ganga) closeby.'

'Whilst staying at the Gyan Mandir *ashram* I find a picture of Swami Shantanand Saraswati, seemingly taken back in the mid-fifties. The picture is stuck on card and framed with some shiny gold tape.'

After his stay at Uttarkashi, Paul Mason again visits Maharishi Ashram at Rishikesh, where he discovers there are many, many dozens of course visitors, and also a contingent of dread locked *sadhus* with their musical instruments.

'The staff of Dhyan Vidhya Peeth refer to the man in charge as 'Swami Ji', seemingly a term of respect for Brahmachari Satyanand. Certainly, his style of teaching is imaginative - on the subject of using a *mantra* to transcend thought and find bliss within, he likens the repetition of the *mantra* to drilling through rock, whilst on the topic of dealing with thoughts that arise in *dhyaan bhavateet* (Transcendental Meditation), he unexpectedly suggests the need to remain passive. I challenge him as to what he means by the word 'passive' - a word which in the west is all-too-often interpreted to mean 'lazy', and he asks me; *'See, a mad man has walked into this room, so, what to do? Do we try to get him out of the room? Do we strike him? No, best to ignore him, just to ignore the madman, and what will he do? He will just walk about, looking at this and looking at that, but if there is no reaction from our side, then eventually he will go out of the door! So, thoughts in meditation we treat like this madman who has walked into this room, we are passive, we do nothing, and then... they go away?'*

Shankaracharya Swami Brahmanand Saraswati
statue sited adjacent to underground lecture hall at Maharishi Ashram, Shankaracharya Nagar

'I question Satyanand on the topic of the *siddhis* - supernatural powers - as Maharishi is rumoured to be conducting experiments into such powers, with meditators being taught various *sutras* in order to enhance their practice. At the mention of *siddhis*, the *brahmachari* suddenly lights up and becomes very animated and wide-eyed, telling me of a *sadhu* who has been staying in one of the beehive *kutir*, and how he, Satyanand, has personally seen the *sadhu* lean back and rise up off the ground. I listen to him with interest, but do not respond, choosing instead to remain passive.'

'There is a notice displayed at the *ashram* which warns in Hindi and English; 'No smoking of Ganja' – my guess is some of the *sadhus* have been getting 'lit up'.

Swami Swaroopanand pictured with Abhinava Vidya Tirth, Niranjana Deva Tirth and Abhinava Sacchidananda Tirth

In 1979 there is a meeting between four Shankaracharyas in which Swami Swaroopananda Saraswati of Jyotir Math meets with Abhinava Vidya Tirth, of Sringeri, Niranjana Deva Tirth, of Puri, Abhinava Saccidananda TIrth, of Dwaraka.

* * * * *

Shankaracharya Swami Shantanand & Brahmachari Satyanand

Swami Vishnudevanand & Shankaracharya Swami Shantanand

On 28th February 1980, Swami Shantanand steps down as Shankaracharya, in favour of Dandi Swami Vishnudevand.

* * * * *

On 23rd June 1980, Sanjay Gandhi, the thirty-three year old politician, son of former Prime Minister Indira Gandhi dies after crashing the plane he is piloting, at Delhi's Safdarjung airport.

* * * * *

Swami Hariharananda, aka Swami Karpatri

Swami Hariharananda, aka Swami Karpatri dies. Known to his devotees as 'Abhinava Shankaracharya' – the 'New Shankaracharya, dies on 7th February 1982, at the age of seventy-seven. His body is submerged in the Ganga on 9th February 1982.

* * * * *

Brahmachari Satyanand, Swami Vasudevanand, Swami Shantanand Saraswati, Maharishi Mahesh Yogi, Brahmachari Nandkishore & Sri Sri Ravi Shankar - Hardwar, 1980

After Swami Shantanand's retirement, Maharishi Mahesh Yogi persuades him to travel abroad, where he involves himself in promoting Transcendental Meditation (TM).

In 1982 Swami Shantanand visits Hong Kong and China, visiting Shanghai, Nanking & Beijing, Moscow and Seelisberg, Switzerland.

On 27th May 1982, at the death of Abhinava Sacchidananda Tirtha, Swami Swaroopanand inherits the title of Shankaracharya of Dwarka.

* * * * *

In March 1983, Swami Shantanand travels abroad again, this time to Africa; touring Kenya, where he visits Nairobi, Mombasa, Kisumu, Nakuru and Eldoret, and goes to Zambia too, visiting Lusaka and Livingstone.

On 31 October 1984, two of Indira Gandhi's bodyguards, Satwant Singh and Beant Singh, shoot her with their service weapons in the garden of the Prime Minister's residence at 1 Safdarjung Road, New Delhi. Indira Gandhi was aged 66.

**Swami Swaroopanand Saraswati and Swami Shantanand Saraswati
at 75th birthday celebration of Swami Brahmanand's oldest disciple, Swami Akhandananda**

In October 1986, in Vrindaban, India, on the occasion of the five-day 75th birthday celebration of Swami Brahmanand's oldest disciple, Swami Akhandananda, which Swami Shantanand and Swami Vishnudevanand attend.

After working as a member of the editorial board of *'Kalyana'* an inspirational magazine produced by Gita Press in Gorakhpur, and also had articles and books published, including his translation, from Sanskrit into Hindi, of Bhagavat Purana, Swami Akhandananda was initiated into *sannyas* by Swami Brahmanand Saraswati in February 1942. In fact, both Swami Akhandananda and Swami Shantanand worked at the Gita Press, and both were disciples of Swami Poornanand Tirth, known as Udiya Baba, until his death in 1948.

Robert Kropinski, a trained TM teacher, seeks an audience with Swami Swaroopanand Saraswati, the Shankaracharya of Dwarka, and is said to have been given a letter of introduction by Swami Prakashanand who is quoted as claiming: - *"I had taken sannyas in a traditional Vedic way from Jagadguru Shankaracharya of Joshimath in 1950 at Allahabad."*

On November 19, 1987, Swami Akhandananda dies and is succeeded by his disciple, Omkaranand Saraswati.

Shankaracharya Swami Vishnudevanand Saraswati

In November 1989 Dandi Swami Vishnudevanand dies, and, according to his Will, Dandi Swami Vasudevanand Saraswati succeeds him as Shankaracharya of Jyotir Math.

In January 1991 His Holiness Shrî Shântânanda Sarasvatî said: *'Liberation is neither a state nor a situation, because all states of being and situations of becoming are related to bondage and ignorance. The moment of total elimination of ignorance is also the moment of enlightenment, which is called liberation. Then all states of being and situations of becoming simply disappear just as all dreams disappear when one is awake. Knowledge only eliminates ignorance. This ignorance is held in the antahkarana (inner mind) and is responsible of fabricating a limited world of its own which can be dissolved by viveka (discrimination). Then there remains the Self in all its glory of eternal existence, constant consciousness and everlasting bliss. Here there is no being and no becoming. It shines but leaves no shadows. Such a soul then needs nothing to do, needs nothing to achieve and needs nothing to defend. But this does not mean that it is dissolved into nothingness. On the contrary it is full and free. ... A liberated antahkarana (a liberated person) does not achieve anything special. It is there as it really is and it can see things and situations as they are complicated in ignorance, and the consciousness in its light uncomplicates the situation and the problem is dissolved. With coloured spectacles of ignorance everything would look as it naturally is. If that coloured spectacle is removed then one can see things as they are. Therefore, with the rise of viveka (discrimination) the coloured spectacles are removed so that things can be seen as they are. Everything looks like a drama and the Self remains witness only, totally detached and totally free. ... The liberated soul makes no claim of being the Brahman for it is the Brahman and will act exactly as Brahman if any complications of ignorance should arise; otherwise it has no reason to need to do anything, since it is always in its glory and freedom. It is rather like an automatic gear in a motorcar, which is capable of responding to any situation, without doing anything.'*

* * * * *

On 21 May 1991, forty-seven year-old ex-Prime Minister Rajiv Gandhi is assassinated in a suicide bombing at Sriperumbudur, near Chennai, in Tamil Nadu, India.

* * * * *

In April of 1992, the Natural Law Party is founded; the brainchild of Maharishi Mahesh Yogi. Former Beatle George Harrison plays a benefit concert at London's Albert Hall.

In the winter of 1992, a transcript of Robert Kropinski's interview with Swami Swaroopanand is published in a newsletter of disaffected TM meditators calling themselves TM-ex. The contents show Swami Swaroopanand to be highly critical of Maharishi Mahesh Yogi and his system of meditation, but since few read the article, as the newsletter has only a small circulation, it does little to dent the reputation of TM, which its proponents are claiming has proven scientific verification.

* * * * *

The succession disputes of Jyotir Math continue and in 1993 or 1994 the situation hots up when it is argued that Swami Swaroopanand cannot be Shankaracharya of more than one *math*. A third claimant stands. Swami Madhavashram, a disciple of Swami Krishnabodhasham. Visiting Joshimath, there are now three alternate signboards to choose from, if you are looking to visit the Shankaracharya of Jyotir Math!

Representatives of Maharishi and the TM organisation attempt to halt publication of a largely positive unofficial biography of Maharishi Mahesh Yogi, but despite the nuisance this causes, the book, '*The Maharishi: The Man Who Gave Transcendental Meditation to the World'* by Paul Mason, is published by Element Book, on schedule. Mick Brown reviews the biography for the *Daily Telegraph*, commenting *'There is a moral here about how attempts to build a heaven on earth all too often end up looking like business opportunities. But the Maharishi always had a winning smile.'* Another reviewer, a Member of Parliament named Gerald Kaufman, writes, *'Paul Mason, though he has practiced TM himself, is no unquestioning worshipper'*. A journalist who is an insider in the TM movement, explains to Maharishi that the author of the biography is clearly very knowledgeable about TM and could easily have disclosed the *mantras* used in TM, had he so wished. He also points out to Maharishi that it is the author's democratic right to write such a book.

HINDUISM TODAY

In 1995 Rajiv Malik travels from New Delhi to Rishikesh, and meets with several *sadhus* who are said to be staying at the Swargashram Trust. The August 1995 issue of *Hinduism Today* contains an article entitled: *'Meet the Real Sadhus of Rishikesh'.*

'Swami Hansa Nand Ji Saraswati said, "I am in this area for the last fifty years, in a cottage for the last 15. My aim in life is to propagate the teachings of Vedanta. I give lectures on Vedanta in my own cottage, and I am also invited elsewhere in prominent ashrams to speak. Vedanta says that you are not this body, but you are pure self, pure consciousness. We must turn inward if we want to be blissful and happy. When you listen to good things you get good thoughts. Therefore try to be in a good company. My guru Karpatri Ji was from Kashi. His message was also to always talk of dharma, devotion and knowledge of the Vedas."

'Swami Narayananand is of the Shankaracharya Sampradaya. He said: "I am seventy-two years old. I lead a very disciplined life. My main message to the people is to go through Holy Scriptures and remember God always. If you live in this way, your life will be happy and blissful."'

'Senior Shankaracharya of Jyotish Peeth dead'

It is reported in *The Hindu* of 7th December 1997, that on Friday 5th December 1997, the former Shankaracharya of Jyotirmath (1953-1980) Swami Shantanand Saraswati has died at the *ashram* at Alopi Bhag, Allahabad. He was born on 16th July 1913, so was eighty-four at his passing.

In 2000, Maharishi Mahesh Yogi awards Tony Abu Nader the title of First Sovereign Ruler of the Global Country of World Peace.

'Dandi Swami' is variously known and referred to as: -
'Dandi Swami Narayananand', 'Narayanananda', 'Narayanand' 'Narayananda',
'Swami Narayana', 'Dandiswami', 'Narayanandaji', 'Swamiji', 'Dandi Swami ji' etc

नारायणानन्द Nārāyaṇānanda

Nārāyaṇa = Supreme Being   ānanda = bliss, ecstasy

*

In late 2000, two visitors from Europe - unknown to one another - travel to Rishikesh and separately meet with Dandi Swami Narayananand Saraswati. Coincidentally, their impressions of the *swami* are later written up and published, in two books, one by Rob H. van Dijk in Dutch as *'Op zoek in India'*, published by Viveki in Holland, the other by Paul Mason, entitled *'Mala - A String of Unexpected Meetings'*. Here Paul describes first meeting Dandi Swami: -

– 5–

'Behind a group of Indians walks an ochre-robed *swami*, lean and tall, his hair tied atop his head in a topknot. In his arms he carries a long object within an orange cloth bag clutched against his chest, which I assume is a wooden staff. I pay him attention purely on the basis of his being a *dandi* or stick-carrying *swami*, since they are rare even amongst holy men. One brief look at his radiant face is enough to convince that this *dandi swami* is definitely a high soul; his eyes reveal deep jewelled pools of light that twinkle and dance. His face immediately reminds me of another's, now seen only in the photographs and paintings, the face of a former Shankaracharya of Jyotir Math who passed away almost fifty years before, whose books I am searching...

I fairly fly into the *dandi swami's* face, gaining his attention.

He appears very pleased as I invoke the name of the departed Shankaracharya, and he rolls his head gently, his eyes sparkling even more than before. With a graceful gesture of the wrist he gently communicates his desire for me to follow him. I am surprised that only with great effort is it possible to keep pace with him. The path we take leads us up the side of the hill, up past many uninhabited beehive-like stone buildings. The *swami* turns to the right and stops at one of the dwellings where he slips off his sandals, unlocks the door and ushers me to go within. Inside he points to a framed photograph placed centrally on a table. It is a rare and beautifully presented photograph of Shankaracharya Swami Brahmanand Saraswati. Reverently, with hands placed together, and I gaze at the portrait. In truth I am stunned that fate should deliver me this opportunity of meeting one of few living disciples of the holy man in the photograph's few living disciples. I study the other two pictures contained in frames upon the table; one is of the Shankaracharya's successor, Swami Shantanand Saraswati whereas the other is of an old man I cannot identify. As I stand musing I am suddenly aware of that the old *swami* is again standing beside me. He chuckles merrily as he points first at himself and then at the photo. But I am thrown into confusion for the picture appears to be of a much older man and I puzzle as to how the *swami* could look so much fresher and younger now than when the photograph was taken.

It occurs to me that I should go and find out whether or not my companion Susan has followed us. I turn to go outside. Coincidentally Susan is just now arriving, and I sense she is unsure how to conduct herself in the company of this aged monk.

'It is the custom to take off one's shoes, as a sign of respect,' I offer. Obligingly she begins to unlace her boots, but the *swami* attracts Susan's attention and beckons for her to go and look at the photographs. She has had insufficient time to unlace her boots and I fret that the *swami* will take offence at her oversight. I wait for the roar! But I worry needlessly, for he appears blissfully unconcerned. I relax and look about me, observing that nailed above the doorway hangs a strip of metal on which is hand-painted the name in Devanagri script 'Dandi Swami Narayanananda Saraswati'.

When Susan rejoins me, I whisper to her: -

'I believe he has achieved the goal of his *sadhana*, his path of spiritual practice. He seems totally at peace, in want of nothing.'

She confides that she has no previous experience whatever of meetings with Indian holy men.

'It is customary to leave a gift,' I whisper to her. 'Have you any fruit, or biscuits perhaps?'

'No, sorry.'

'Some small offering, we could leave those blossoms you're holding.'

'Yes, fine.'

Swami Ji settles down, become seated on a wooden table outside his dwelling and makes himself comfortable, and, by gestures, facial expressions and endearing chuckles the *swami* puts us at ease. He sorts through some papers and seems pleased to show me pages of an air letter, possibly several air letters, from someone in Holland. Evidently, the *swami* has been staying here long enough for someone to establish communication with him here. He takes a piece of white chalk and writes a word in Hindi on a chalkboard

मौन

The word is *'maun'*, meaning a vow of silence. Thus is explained his lack of conversation, however, he appears happy enough to write simple answers to my few questions.

I mention Jyotir Math and can't help remarking: -

'It seems as though this meeting is a message for us to travel to the mountains and go to Joshimath,' I laugh. Susan grins her agreement.

I find myself again sobbing gently and find myself incapable of speaking much before tears well up. I feel compelled to explain to the *swami* that since visiting a poor man locally I have been taken with this condition for some days. Swami Ji begins to write on the chalkboard again and I puzzle the meaning of the Devanagari letters. Spelled out they form two seemingly unfamiliar words

वेरी गूद

'V-E-R-I-I G-U-U-D-A'.

At first I don't get the meaning, and then...

'VERY GOOD?' I ask, shaking with mirth as I interpret the meaning. 'Really? Good, good. Thank you Swami Ji.'

For several minutes I bask in the lightness and good humour of this saintly man. Then, when I sense I should take my leave, I feel a strong compulsion to signal my very great respect for the *swami*. I find myself not only lowering my head as I intend, but suddenly and quite involuntarily throwing myself upon the dusty ground, my arms outstretched to touch his feet. I feel his hands hover behind my head as if in blessing.

Positively glowing, I accompany Susan away from the *swami*'s presence.

'I've never thrown myself at the feet of anyone in my life!' I confide to her, 'But then I've never met such a man before. We have been blessed indeed. Did you notice how when he moves it is so graceful, as if there were not a bone in his body?'

Susan smiles.

'As we are up here, would you like to take a walk about the *ashram*?' I suggest pointing to a grove of palm trees.

A man's voice comes as if from nowhere: -

'No, no, you should not go.'

We walk on but only to find our way obstructed.

'It soon dark is,' he informs us. 'Tomorrow you are coming. Yes tomorrow come again.'

So Susan and I retrace our steps downhill and after but just a few minutes we notice the sun already disappearing from view, leaving washes of red streaks in the bright blue evening sky. In the short time it takes to re-join the main concrete path into the village darkness descends very rapidly.

'He was right you know, we would have been wandering in the dark,' I admit.

Entering the village, the glittering bright lights of the shops offer a dazzling spectacle. The pretty lights reflect and sparkle on the many colourful goods displayed there.

Susan marvels at the sight, as I do I, for it is as if everything has been brushed by magic. The sounds enchant too and the air hangs with sweet pungent aromas, incense mixed with the smell of fresh citrus fruits. I am minded that the name Swargashram means '*ashram* of Heaven' or '*ashram* of Paradise'. I imagine that a marketplace in paradise could hold no greater feast for the senses. All-at-once both Susan and myself hear the sound of beautiful music floating up from the riverside. As we go to investigate we find a swathe of pilgrims celebrating evening prayers accompanied by some very fine musicians, the sounds of voices and instruments being routed through a powerful public address system. Amongst the amassed crowds I see a concentration of dozens of spluttering orange flames emanating from a brass holder, it is carried and passed over the swaying singing congregation gathered, packed tightly together on the steps leading down to the Ganga. And there, amidst the rushing waters, a massive statue of Lord Shiva sits facing them. From all directions come flashes of light, as cameras capture these magic moments.

A few days later, Dutchman Rob van Dijk encounters Dandi Swami Narayananand, and later describes his feelings in his book 'Op zoek in India': -

'The sudden encounter with this man is particularly moving. I fix my gaze on his figure and his movements. It is clear that the emotionally charged atmosphere is surely linked to his presence and not to anything else. It is really exciting.'

Dandi Swami, Rob van Dijk & his wife Willeke in October 2000

Let us enjoy some excerpts from Rob H. van Dijk's diary, of his second journey to India, contained in 'Op zoek in India', published by Viveki in 2010 (and translated here into English courtesy of Paul van Oyen). Paul says of Rob: - 'He was an ardent follower of the teachings of Adi Shankara and his successors. As a student of School voor Filosofie he was well informed about HH Shrî Shântânanda Sarasvatî, Shankarâcârya of Jyotir Math.'

* * * * *

Excerpts from Rob H. van Dijk's account of his second journey to India

October 2000
Mahesh Yogi Ashram

The third *ashram* that I visited in Rishikesh is situated on the other side of the river Ganges. It didn't look very appealing because it was not used any more. It had been the Mahesh Yogi Ashram and acquired some fame because The Beatles and other well-known people from the West had stayed there.

.....

In my opinion Maharishi was a rather special person. I highly regarded the Maharishi because of his translation of the first six chapters of the Bhagavad Gîtâ together with a commentary that gives the Western reader far reaching insights. As far as the TM movement as such is concerned there seems to be a lot of marketing and commercially motivated activities around the TM-movement causing a great deal of money streaming through it. Even in the West Maharishi had to face criticism and opposition and therefore, for me personally, I do not find him attractive as a *guru*.

However, I am firmly determined to find, in some way or other, *satsangs* that would suit me. It would be too absurd if it would be impossible to find some form of *advaita* teaching in the cradle of *advaita* itself. We are in India and, what is more, we are in Rishikesh. So I decided to search for the *ashram* of Maharishi on the other side of the riverbank. It is only possible to get there by a hanging bridge for pedestrians or by a ferryboat. Cars cannot get there, not even a rickshaw. So we take the ferryboat and go to the other side. We turn right and find ourselves in the middle of many small shops and quite a number of different *ashrams* alongside the riverbank. We move on and on until we leave the last shops and the last huts of 'the poor people' behind us. We walk on until the end of the road because of the rock formations that rise up vertically from the Ganges riverbank. People told us that some holy men, *sadhus*, live here in caves in the rocky hills. Several times we were told that the Mahesh Yogi Ashram has been closed and dissolved. We were also told that there is nothing to see or to experience. Here the road ends up as a cul-de-sac. We meet some *sadhus* and they confirm the dissolution of Mahesh Yogi Ashram but they do say that there still one *mahâtma* living in the grounds in complete solitude. Unnecessary to go there. But why is there this lingering determination not to give up, why do I continue my search? Is it simple obstinacy? Taking a side path I find myself suddenly in front of an iron gate that must have been the main entrance to the *ashram*. The whole area is like a monkey kingdom. Both my wife Willeke and driver Ramesh urge me to return and stop going any further. But my curiosity has been aroused and I keep telling them 'let me just have another look around this corner'.

It is no problem to side step the iron gate because the wall on the right hand has collapsed. So we move on and walk towards a rather steep hillock and there is another, second, gate that is open. Now we look towards a wide green that is now turning into a jungle. At the far end we notice someone walking next to the ruins of a larger building. Driver Ramesh walks to him and starts talking to him. The man in question is the caretaker of the place and he is willing to introduce us to the *mahâtma* who lives in one of the stupas on the right hand side of the path. They are a kind of cupola, like a stupa, and they are built from small and larger pebbles set in cement. Each stupa has a first floor of about three square metres. On the ground floor the stupa measures some six square metres. We were told that Maharishi also occupied one these stupas.

First meeting with my *guru*
23.10.2000

I notice the *mahâtma* from a distance: a slimly built man, strikingly tall and wrapped up in an orange skirt like thing. I get a lump in my throat but I know not from what. Clearly it is a special moment but I do not know why. Is it the atmosphere? Is it the presence of the *mahâtma*? Is it the information that The Beatles were here before? My mind is racing around and comes up with anything without giving a real insight or understanding. It certainly is an emotionally charged moment. I can see something but I do not know what. I have seen so many of these orange coloured robes. The sudden encounter with this man is particularly moving. I fix my gaze on his figure and his movements. It is clear that the emotionally charged atmosphere is surely linked to his presence and not to anything else. It is really exciting. The next moment we are introduced to the one inhabitant of this huge *ashram*: Dandî Svâmî Narâyanânanda. A *mahâtma* of very few words. He is surely not standoffish but neither is he friendly. Rather neutral. He begs us in silence to sit down on a stone bench in front of his stupa. He also appoints every one of us to a place. He himself will be seated on a low wooden table. Ramesh acts as interpreter. A thin placemat is put in the middle of a stone bench and I am invited to sit on it. Willeke will sit next to me. Until then he has not spoken one word. The one sound he makes is a kind of clicking sound with the tongue behind his teeth if he asks for attention or if he shakes 'no'. It clears the atmosphere which assumes a kind of serenity and which is clearly special. Yet it is also exciting and it feels as if I have some kind of stage fright. Ramesh translates what the Svâmî has written on a small slate and what the caretaker has to say.

The *mahâtma* has not spoken a word for the last four months, as a spiritual exercise [known as *maun*], and he plans to continue for another two months. He has a very friendly face full of expression, which is not surprising if one has desisted from speaking for such a long time. I tell him that Willeke and I come from Holland and that in the town where we live there is a TM-siddha village. I also tell him that Maharishi lives in Holland, in a former Roman Catholic monastery that he is planning to take down to make room from a brand new building based on Vedic architecture. However there has been a court case and the court decided that the building should be preserved as an example of a catholic monastery. As a result Maharishi plans to move to the U.S. It seems that the *mahâtma* is well informed about these developments. He even understands my English. But his answers are chalked on the slate in Hindi.

It becomes increasingly clear that this man is not just a *svâmî* like so many others. I was very pleased to discover that Svâmî Narâyanânanda knew Shrî Brahmânanda Sarasvatî, Shankarâcârya of Joshimath from 1941 until 1953 when he passed away. His successor was Shrî Shântânanda Sarasvatî. When I made it clear to him that Willeke and I got our understanding of the wisdom of *advaita* from him (through the School voor Filosofie) he became, in turn, very pleased. He said that Shrî Shântânanda Sarasvatî was his *guru*. He went into his little stupa-hut and came back with a somewhat tattered photograph of Shrî Shântânanda Sarasvatî in a nice frame. He beckoned us to come inside. Shoes out, of course. We see three photographs in their frames of Shrî Brahmânanda Sarasvatî, of Shrî Shântânanda Sarasvatî and one of himself, Shrî Narâyanânanda Sarasvatî. It is clear to me that if any one would be able to explain the circumstances of the resignation of Shrî Shântânanda Sarasvatî, it would be Shrî Narâyanânanda.

When I approach the subject of the succession in Jyoshimath and the three contestants to the title the *svâmî* looks at me surprised. But I am surprised too because this is the first time that I get confirmation of three contestants to the title of Shankarâcârya of the North (Jyoshimath). He writes their names down on his little slate: Svarupânanda, Madhavashrama and Vasudevânanda. When I ask him who in his opinion is *the* Shankrâcârya of Jyoshimath he convincingly and without hesitation answers: Shrî Vasudevânanda Sarasvatî. I hardly dare to put my next question: why are you so convinced? The answer was short and clear: Shrî Vasudevânanda was a follower of Shrî Shântânanda Sarasvatî. I see a row of further question coming up in the mind but they also pass away and dissolve. I had read an informative paper on the succession issue in Jyoshimath with a broad legal analysis of the situation. All three contestants have their point to validate their claim. The writer weighs the pros and cons against each other and comes to the conclusion that in his opinion Shrî Svarûpânanda has the best 'papers'. Still I found this way of discussing this issue not very convincing and not appealing. I couldn't point out why not and why I did not feel convinced.

But now *Svâmîjî* made a real point and said that conviction does not arise from argumentation and proving your point. Proofs do not arise on the basis of argumentation. Conviction arises from within. Doubts will dissolve from within. The 'yes but ...' questions do not arise any more . Now I hear the voice of authority and what else can I do but to watch how my arguments gradually dissolve.

This meeting was for me a really joyful experience. Here is a man who I had been looking for during such a long time. I would have loved to sit next to him in silence. There are no more desires. I am so happy. But at a certain moment it is clear that it was enough. Even I saw that this was the case.

....

– 6 –

Mantra's given by my *guru*
24.10.2000

At four o'clock in the afternoon I go on my own to Dandi Svâmî Narayânânanda Sarasvatî. His name is nicely written on a nameplate in red Sanskrit lettering next to the door of his *stupa.*

दण्डी स्वामी नारायणानन्द सरस्वती

नारायणानन्द कुटीर

शंकराचार्यनगर

ऋषिकेश

Dandi Swami Narayananand Saraswati
Narayananand Kutir
Shankaracharya Nagar
Rishikesh

Our conversation this time is about meditation. He wishes to know which *mantras* I am using. I give him my *mantra* consisting of one word: *râm.* Then he starts to write on his slate. Three words. Fortunately I am able to read Sanskrit and pronounce it. I write the words in my writing pad and he tells me to pronounce the words. Every time he points at one of the words and in this way the particular *mantra* is pronounced. This is repeated a number of times. In this way we go through five small sentences until I know them by heart and until he is satisfied with my pronunciation. It is a strange situation: someone who doesn't want to speak because of his vow of silence and who can only nod with his head is teaching a *mantra* to someone who is reading Sanskrit like a small child. *Svâmîjî* points out on his slate that these are five basic *mantra's, namah mantras* that were given to him by his *guru,* Shrî Shântânanda Sarasvatî. They are *bija mantras,* seed forms. He advises me to use them because I am, like him, a follower of Shrî Shântânanda Sarasvatî. When taking leave of him I want to give him some money, which he refuses to accept, until I tell him that it is for the *guru.*

I feel really happy while I walk back to the hotel along the banks of the river Ganges. I realise that this was a very special meeting and I enjoyed every moment of it. I look around and sit down for a moment on the pebbles on the riverbank. My mind has come to rest and I only notice some thoughts that come and go through the mind. It is like the sunlit surroundings where everything moves along quietly. There are the possession-free *sadhus* who sit quietly together in small groups. There is the river that streams quietly along. My mind is just a reflection of all this. No desires, no ambitions, no stress whatsoever. Here is the fullness of enjoyment. One with the surroundings.

About Shankarâcârya Shântânanda
26.10.2000

My third visit to the Svâmî is once more together with Willeke. We took some fruits with us for the Svâmî and I asked a few questions about the origin of Joshimath, which is the seat of the Shankarâcârya of the North. The so-called voluntary resignation of Shrî Shântânanda Sarasvatî as Shankarâcârya of the North had everything to do with politics. Svâmî Narayânânanda refuses to go further into this. He explains that the question is too complicated and that it all happened too long ago. Suddenly he gets up and goes inside his stupa. I hear him opening the door of his cupboard and closing it. Then he comes out again and hands a yellowish booklet of twelve pages to me. On the cover is a small formal photograph of His Holiness Shrî Shântânanda Sarasvatî on his throne with a tiger hide in front. The text is in Hindi. Svâmîjî points to a few sentences that I can pronounce but the meaning escapes me. Is here an explanation of Shrî Shântânanda's resignation in 1980 as Shankarâcârya? I cannot figure out what it means. On the last page there is a chart as I have seen earlier with the qualities of the four different seats (*pîthams*). When we leave he will give us this booklet as a present.

Svâmî Narayânânanda vaguely remembers Leon MacLaren (the senior tutor and schoolmaster of the School of Economic Science in London and of the various schools abroad including School voor Filosofie in Holland. But the name of Dr Roles of the Study Society, London is well known to him and he is apparently pleased to hear this name mentioned. He also knows Svâmî Prabodhânanda in Varanasi. I try to persuade him to write a small message in my writing pad for Svâmî Prabodhânanda but he refuses and it is clear that this name does not kindle great enthusiasm with him. I do not know why and I do not wish to ask any further. As usual, India may be a 'free' country but below the surface there are many fixed ideas and likes and dislikes that seem to limit the freedom appreciably.

When we took leave of Svâmîjî he gave us a banana and a nectarine from the fruit we took with us for him.

More information about Shrî Shântânanda
28.10.2000

Shrî Shantânanda Sarasvatî resigned as Shankarâcârya of Jyotir Math in 1980 at the insistence of a special commission. I presumed this already but neither the caretaker nor Svâmî Narâyanânanda were willing to provide any further details. It was clear that they would not appreciate any further questioning. As far as I know Shrî Shantânanda Sarasvatî had never been abroad, outside India, but according to Shrî Narâyanânanda his *guru* made a trip abroad in 1980. He went to China, Holland and England. Surprising information! In England he would have visited Dr Roles. Although both my hosts clearly knew the name of Leon MacLaren it was also clear that he did not leave a great impression behind in contrast to Dr Roles. According to both my hosts Shrî Shantânanda was a very special person, a vessel full of wisdom and knowledge both intellectually and spiritually. They lived both for some time in the *ashram* of Shrî Shantânanda Sarasvatî in Allahabad. Svâmî Narâyanânanda studied for more than fifteen years the Bhagavad Gîtâ and the Upanishad under his *guru*. Svâmîjî was one of the senior disciples of Shrî Shantânanda Sarasvatî just as Shrî Vasudevânanda, the present Shankarâcârya.

A letter of introduction for Svâmî Vasudevânanda

Would Shrî Narâyanânanda perhaps be willing to write a letter of introduction for Shrî Vasudevânanda? This is the question that I asked through the caretaker. I couldn't help asking it, even if I had the intention not to do so. The answer was an unexpected 'of course'. Svâmî Narâyanânanda was getting ready for writing the required letter. Would I get, after all, access to Svâmî Vasudevânanda in this roundabout way? Then I am asked: 'what is the subject you would like to raise with Shrî Vasudevânanda'? The first word that comes up in my mind is 'meditation'. The atmosphere suddenly changes completely. The caretaker's reaction is as if a wasp stung him. The Svâmî immediately puts down his pen and removes his writing pad. The caretaker answers: 'no, that will not be possible'. I am rather confounded and ask 'why not?' A simple question receives a simple answer: 'Shrî Vasudevânanda doesn't know enough about meditation'. This is the domain of Shrî Shantânanda Sarasvatî, but he passed away and meditation is now the domain of Maharishi Mahesh Yogi. The caretaker steps in and takes a defensive approach. He acts as a screen between Svâmî Narâyanânanda and myself. If I wish to know more about meditation I should go to Delhi and visit the headquarters of the TM movement. He even gives me the full address.

My argument that our organisation in Holland, the *School voor Filosofie*, has become rather out of control on this point does not help in any way. It is no reason for writing a letter of introduction to Svâmî Vasudevânanda. Could Svâmî Narâyanânanda answer some questions about meditation? Even then the caretaker answers negative, stating that Svâmîjî doesn't know enough about meditation. I am flabbergasted. Not even fifteen minutes ago the caretaker was quick enough to tell me that the one thing Svâmîjî is keeping up is meditation. I try to press on but the staunch answer is to visit TM headquarters in Delhi at their address as given. Now I turn directly to Svâmî Narâyanânanda and the caretaker is forced to translate. Could Svâmîjî tell us more about the point of concentration during meditation? It could be the area of the heart, the tip of the nose or the point between the eyes. Is this right? If so, could you recommend one of these points and what are the differences? The first answer is that there are five points of concentration: heart, throat, forehead and the crown of the head. The choice is a personal one. Svâmî Narâyanânanda recommends the crown. He looks heavenly and enlightened when saying this. The second answer is that there are seven *chakras*. During meditation one moves upward from bottom to the top and then back again. It doesn't become very clear if one runs through this circular movement from bottom to top and back again in one half hour or that one runs through this circular movement in one breath. Maybe both ways are possible.

It is clear that the caretaker is not pleased with the way the conversation is going. Svâmîjî is writing all kinds of things on his slate and he points towards me and towards himself. His writing is clearly meant for me but when I ask for a translation the caretaker says to wait a little longer and in the end I am completely ignored. He simply stops translating.

Out of control

I have the strong impression that something is carefully and hermetically closed off as something unmentionable. On our return to Rishikesh I mention this to Willeke. What am I doing? What am I looking for? Now I am feeling as if I am also 'out of control'. To me it is clear that staying in *ashrams*, which looked so appealing when I was in the Netherlands, is not my path. Staying in the presence of Svâmî Narâyanânanda, in a rather desolate spot and staying in stillness and silence is different and is appealing. But why am I posing silly questions? What do I really want to know? What *do I really want*?

Willeke rightly points out to me that such questions 'can only be solved by meditation'. During evening-meditation the figure of Svâmî Prabhodhânanda in Varanasi comes up and how he does his rituals every day with great care and devotion. That picture often rises up in my mind and I relate it to religion. I want to know what religion is and what is the essence of service to God. To me the rituals that are so important to many Indians seem rather unnecessary and irrelevant but now I suddenly understand in a flash that this is a key. Religious rituals without a specific and material purpose are free from desires and demands. Indeed, they free one from desires and demands. Would this be true? I hardly dare to believe it. But what is the purpose of spiritual organisations such as the School voor Filosofie? In the end they also bring discord and quarrels. I am not referring to the first years for a spiritual aspirant because for such newcomers these organisations are very efficient and well equipped. But after many years, what then? Should one stay loyal to one organisation or should one go one's own way? I can only say that I lost the way, Why learn Sanskrit or Hindi? Is that necessary for liberation, *moksha*?

Taking leave of Svâmî Narâyanânanda
28.10.2000

The next day Willeke and I return to Svâmî Narâyanânanda in order to take leave from him. On our way to him we buy some fruits for him but before we reach the *ashram* we meet him on the way. So we walk to the *ashram* together. For a man in his seventies he climbs the hill amazingly quickly without gasping for air. He is a beautiful person, tall, slimly built, playful eyes and a big smile. His movements are refined and yet resolute.

We sit down in front of his stupa and I show him the letter that I had written on the previous evening. He smiles and is pleased. He corrects some of the Sanskrit that I had written and then he enquires after meditation. I tell him that I have no trouble in finding the points of concentration except for the crown of the head. He writes on his slate: slowly, slowly it will be alright. Enjoy your trip through India, be patient, patient. When we take leave from him he gives us again some fruits but it nearly fails because a large group of cheeky monkeys moves along and nothing is really safe from their grabbing and incredibly quick fingers. Svâmî Narâyanânanda must continuously threaten them with a long stick to keep them at a distance.

We depart and wave to him from a distance but to no avail. The wise man gives his attention to his own things without any fuss. I regard this as a sign of wisdom: a physical goodbye should not take longer than necessary and therefore one turns the mind and attention to the next thing and to the order of the day.

When we reach the banks of the river Ganges we see how the sun is settling at the other side of the river. A beautiful bright orange orb. We decide to meditate on the riverbank. Then we walk to the ferryboat and have dinner in a small restaurant on the other side of the river.

* * * * *

Paul van Oyen: - 'Both visitors (and others too) were highly impressed by the sense of presence of this *Svâmi*. He seemed a real *Svâmi* in the literal sense of the word *'Svâmi'*: someone who is master of himself or someone who is firmly rooted in his (or hers) essential being. In theory this should apply to any *sannyâsin* or, indeed, to any *yogi* but in the course of time these definitions have been widened to include many non-essential features that in fact have obscured the true meaning and stature of these imposing figures. Depending on the intensity of their personal discipline and the quality of their *tapas* (ascetic attitudes) the *real svâmis* and *sannyâsins* will belong to the very upper stages of human wisdom. They are highly evolved human beings. Their basic feature is the dominant presence at all times of a *sattvic* nature, followed by various degrees of insight, understanding, love, detachment and all other human virtues. A *sattvic* quality is a quality of light and intelligence, of a highly developed emotional capacity and, above all, of a peaceful attitude. Non-violence is a direct corollary of such a nature. Such a person lives in the region of light. Only in light it is possible so see clearly and to differentiate between clean and dirty, good and bad, beautiful and ugly and so on. It is no longer a matter of convention to differentiate between good and bad, right and wrong. Such a person sees a situation as it really is and observes the facts as they are without falling prey to the delusion of sentimentality. Such a person knows no fear because all fear comes from darkness and ignorance. He is steady, upright, unhesitant and has a great clarity. He is a person of great caliber and power and is filled with courage and hope. Wherever such a person moves about, he (or she) will bring light and a situation is transformed into clear light.'

– 7 –

On Thursday 9th November, after meditation, Paul Mason makes a return visit to the abandoned *ashram* where Dandi Swami Narayananand lives, but on arriving at Shankaracharya finds the *swami's kutir* padlocked. However, he easily slips into conversation with Mr. Thakur, a gently spoken Indian who lives on site with his family.

Mr. Thakur

'The two of us chat awhile, and as we talk he takes me for a walk about the grounds of the former Academy of Meditation. He asks me if I am a doctor. I frown. He asks excitedly, whether or not I am a friend of 'The Doctor'. Clearly, the doctor is a visitor from abroad. Dr Roles? Doctor who?

It is clear that Mr. Thakur does not wish to be seen as a common squatter for he takes time to impress upon me that he works here taking care of 'initiation work' (initiation being a term used by the TM organisation to mean instruction in meditation). In addition to teaching TM he also claims to deal with 'management' (which evidently includes the dual tasks of watchdog and reception committee).

'At this time all activities are closed here,' he informs me. 'New buildings is here after one year.' But it is all too evident that no construction work has yet been started. Perhaps he senses my doubts?

'Permit extension after some time,' he assures himself.

It is difficult to comprehend why anyone would have the authority to demolish any of these buildings, for none of them are particularly old. 'But if the buildings really are to be pulled down what will take their place?'

'Good Vedic gardens and guest house for foreigns.'

'No longer an *ashram* then?'

'No,' he states, evidently uncomfortable at the thought.

I change the subject: - 'I have come to see Dandi Swami Narayanand. He was not in his *kutir*. Do you think he is coming back soon?'

'Yes, you will be seeing him. He is very *guru*, he has enlightenment!' he comments rather matter-of-factly, as if reading the contents of a can of food. Enlightenment must be commonplace in these parts or for what other reason would he make such light work of the subject?

Suddenly a commotion erupts. An adult *langur* attempts to tear the paper bag I'm carrying from my grasp, and in doing so spills several fruits to the ground. The cunning creature had sidled up completely unnoticed.

'Wow, that was clever, he came out of nowhere!' I exclaim with amazement as the *langur* scampers away to the trees.

'Eighty, - ninety monkeys here all the time. They are very criminal,' he replies informs me in a concerned voice.

We have arrived at a red and white-pinnacled structure, which contains a Shivalinga, a shrine to Shivashakti. My companion shyly asks me to take a photograph of himself and his daughter. As they stand posing, a young Indian woman emerges from a nearby building stepping into the bright sunlight. She is the girl's mother and she quickly declines her husband's request for her to join them in the photograph, excusing herself saying she instead wishes to perform *puja*, a religious ceremony, and so slips away. Father and daughter pose beside the sacred *lingam*. The camera clicks and whirrs successfully, though with concern I observe that the batteries are running extremely low.

'Perhaps the *swami* has by now returned,' I suggest. 'I think I will check one time more before I go.'

'Yes we go to him now. I think he is returned. Maybe.'

Leaving the *ashram* compound, we walk together to the gate adjacent to the holyman's rooms. I do not see anyone there, but I notice that the door to the *kutir* is ajar and a pair of sandals lie beside it, which would seem to suggest he is back. There is a flicker of light amongst illuminating the shadowed entrance and all-at-once the orange robed Dandi Swami is standing directly before us. He beckons us, his bright eyes flashing a greeting of welcome. And again I am awed to be in his presence for he radiates such a concentrated atmosphere of inner strength and well-being. My companion speaks up, telling of the photography session. I wonder at him, that he bothers to share such information with the holyman. When the *swami* hears tell of the photo-shoot he communicates to me by gestures that I ought to note my companions contact details. A very practical suggestion if I am to send a copy of the printed photograph when the film has been developed. With his permission I use the *swami's* pen to take down the man's address. Swami Ji is also quick to note that the address I am given by the man, Mr. Thakur, lacks a 'pin number', or postal code. He writes this for me on his chalkboard and holds it aloft, chuckling to himself as he does so. He appears to take an almost childlike delight in involving himself in the world of administration; Mr. Thakur's designated work.

Still holding the pen, I think decide to take the opportunity to commit the holyman's likeness to paper. I attempt to sketch him and as I do so I listen to Mr. Thakur as he translates the Hindi words on the *swami's* chalkboard.

'Swami Ji, silence he makes for four months. At this time he will speak after two days.'

Mr. Thakur sounds puzzled as he tells me: - 'Swami is also saying he knows you before,' he says sounding very surprised. I assume the *swami* is referring to our prior meeting, though I am not certain, for in India it is not uncommon for people to casually refer to former lifetimes! I contemplate this truth as I continue to draw.

But soon I abandon my crude sketch and surprise myself as I summon up the courage to ask if I might use my camera instead. Narayanananda Ji chuckles and casually unties his topknot, letting fall a shower of long silvering hair to tumble over his shoulders.

Mr. Thakur & Dandi Swami Narayananand Saraswati

Taking up the long cloth-covered 'dandi' staff he then seats himself cross-legged on the wooden bench and motions for Mr. Thakur to pull up a chair and join him for the photograph. The camera whirrs, the job is done. Mr. Thakur does not stay.

Left alone with the *swami* I am tempted to stretch my luck a little and ask if I can take one more shot. Again he chuckles, twinkles his eyes and waggles his heavily bearded head in assent. As he sits he presents the definitive image of the cheery self-realised *guru*. In an instant I imagine his taking to the stage at a Rock music venue - imagining the crowds taking to him very easily. I feel inspired to move my position, to crouch down in front of him. I compose the picture; taking care to include his wooden sandals. The shaded scene, dappled with morning sunlight, perhaps only needs but a bounce of flash and I am concerned that in waiting for the weak battery to power-up the flash attachment, I might be testing the *swami's* patience in keeping him waiting. I hold fire for just a while longer. I raise my eyes from the camera; Swami Ji flickers his eyebrows, apparently in approval signalling that the time is right. Pressing the button my instincts tell me the photograph is perfect.

Dandi Swami Narayananand Saraswati - Thursday 9th November 2000
photo: Premanand Paul Mason

I put away the camera and return to the *swami's* side, to place beside him my offering of fruits and the few flowering purple blooms that formerly adorned the street vendor's barrow. The *swami's* hands hover over the fruits a moment, as if in blessing. He gestures for me to sit on the blanket that he spreads by his side. As I sit quietly with him, my mind flickers and splutters into liveliness, I become awake to the very great opportunity this meeting affords me, for it is not everyday one has the chance to sit in the presence of such a man. I suspect that whatever people mean by the words 'enlightened' and *'guru'*, he personifies them.

I begin asking him a few questions: -

'Swami Ji, should I continue my meditations?'

He answers with an affirmative roll of his head. This surprises me for I half expect him to advise me to perform some different practice instead. On a previous visit to India I met with another monk of Jyotir Math monastery who appeared quite offish about the need for inner meditation, saying 'Here it not necessary to meditate.' Also when I sat for meditation in Trotakacharya Gupha, a cave near to the monastery, a monk there voiced certain discouragement.

'I also wish to teach meditation, is this alright?'

Again the *swami* offers a very positive reaction.

In his graceful responses to my earnest enquiries I derive incredible strength and support for my spiritual aspirations. My self-assurance grows by the moment. As I sit glowing with the satisfaction at having gained the *dandi swami's* permission and approval, the memory of my recent hands-on healing treatment springs to mind. Without hesitation I decide to ask his opinion about such practices.

'Recently I have been given Reiki,' I explain. 'I would like to show you what happened.' I lay myself down prone on the trodden earth before him and proceed to re-enact some of the more sensational aspects of the session, the twists, turns, jerks and sudden bursts of rapid deep breathing. As I replay the dramatic highlights of the session he responds with nods, smiles and rolls his head from side to side. When I have finished my re-enactment he demonstrates for me a breathing exercise, indicating that it will be useful for me to practice. Drawing myself up, I practice by his example and then remain sitting cross-legged before him, assuming the role of pupil. I have observed that *gurus* seem always seem to seat themselves higher than their visitors do, I had thought it customary for them to do so.

By gestures the *swami* makes it obvious that he does not wish for me to remain seated at his feet, but that I should return to my place beside him on the rug he has laid for me there. I return without delay. I feel no desire to speak further, since, as he has answered my questions, there is nothing better to do other than sit in the quietness and enjoy the gift of his graceful smiling companionship. After some long time spent enjoying blissful moments with the Swami Ji I notice his manner subtly alters and he now raises his strong eyebrows and for a moment the bright red *tilak* and horizontal lines of sandalwood that grace his brow almost resemble a frown. Springing to his feet he takes up a piece of cloth and, with skilful slight of hand worthy of a seasoned conjurer, he deftly uses it to cover and gather up my offerings. Whereupon, a thwarted bandit monkey scampers away to regain the cover of the jungle, it's schemes foiled again.

'What should I do next?' I ask the *swami*, hoping for some last spiritual guidance before leaving him. Without a moment's hesitation he takes up his chalkboard and writes in clear sweeping motions. My eyes light on three words in particular: -

'*Snan lata kumbh*' - *snan lata* I take to refer to bathing, *kumbh*, I vaguely recall as meaning a pot. He therefore appears to be advising me to undertake some sort of ritual bath. Perhaps he is advising me to become an ascetic?

'Where must I go?' I ask of him.

'Prayag,' he writes. Prayag I know is the term for the meeting of two rivers as found in local place names such as Devaprayag and Rudraprayag, which I have visited. It is also the ancient name for the city of Allahabad.

'Allahabad?' I query.

He grins almost conspiratorially, as if divulging a great secret.

'Brahma Nivas, Alopi Bhag,' he writes. It is clear now, for the name of the monastery and its address are contained in an area of my memory, which has suddenly, became activated. Swami Narayananand is inviting me to go to the monastery in Allahabad.

'Shankaracharya Ashram!' I marvel.

He smiles, waggles his head and nods again, crinkling his eyes, squeezing rays of his inner light to scatter about him.

I ask him when I should travel to Allahabad.

This time he uses no chalkboard; only he uses his eyes and simple hand gestures. Circling with his finger he points first to his own head and then to mine. I understand, at least I think I understand. I believe he means me to think about it. It is for me to decide.

As I stand ready to leave, he bids me wait a moment and goes to select a piece of fruit, which he presents to me. As on my previous visit, as I depart I reach to touch his feet and as I do so I feel his hands linger behind my head. As he blesses me, I hear a sound issue from him, similar to the sound of the hissing of a snake, then again all is silent again. Respectfully I bow my head and place my hands together.

'Jay Shri Gurudev,' I say, meaning 'Glory be to blessed Gurudev', a customary greeting in praise of his *guru*.

I back away from his presence and as I do so I notice his eyes appear to narrow slightly. But as I fervently desire one last look into the infinite depths his wide-open eyes, I pause longer, expectantly. Although I believe he understands my unspoken wish, he remains steadfast without movement, offering to me a last silent instruction - that, for whatever reason or however well intentioned, it is futile to attempt exertion of one's own willpower over that of an enlightened master.'

– 8 –

Whilst staying in Swargashram, I also become friends with another *sadhu*, who calls himself Roopanand. I mention his name to Dandi Swami, and tell him this *swami* is living locally. Dandi Swami becomes very animated and excited, and I get the distinct impression he thinks I am mispronouncing the name, and that he thinks it is Shankaracharya Swami Swaroopanand who I have met with.

* * * * *

Before leaving India, Paul Mason feels inspired to write a note to Maharishi Mahesh Yogi. Whilst on his way to post the letter he encounters Dandi Swami Narayananand who shows much interest in the unsealed aerogramme, reading it attentively, waggling his head to show he understands its contents. Here are some extracts from the letter: -

नमस्ते जी [Namaste Ji]

Some years ago I felt inspired to write your life story, primarily as a means of passing on some of the rare insights that you have shared. I also felt compelled to write your story at the inspiration of your guru Shankaracharya Swami Brahmanand Saraswati who allegedly encouraged openness in matters of personal biography and news of interest to the general public.

'Since I am currently preparing 'The Maharishi: The Biography of the Man Who Gave Transcendental Meditation to the World' for re-publication, this is a particularly appropriate time to consider revisions and fresh material. I therefore invite your comments.

जय गुरुदेव [Jay Guru Dev]

'The letter also mentions Swami Narayananand - it is good that I now know the *swami* is fully appraised of my link with Maharishi.'

* * * * *

'I am unsure whether to take Dandi Swami's advice, to go to the Kumbh Mela festival at Allahabad, but I return to Rishikesh in December 2000, with half a mind to take my family to the Kumbh. We meet with Dandi Swami on the riverside path at Swargashram, and he greets Ben, my youngest son who is just days away from celebrating his thirteenth birthday, and he squeezes his cheeks between thumbs and forefingers, affectionately, rather in the manner of a grandfather. Kathy - Ben's mum - watches on and seems quite at-ease with Dandi Swami, and he with her, quite naturally.'

Dandi Swami Narayananand Saraswati - 2001

– 9 –

Excerpts from Rob H. van Dijk's diary relating to his third journey to India

April 2001

(Rob van Dijk returns to Rishikesh)

.... Now it is time to go to Svâmî Narâyanânanda. Outside it is very hot. I never experienced such intensive heat. My mouth is continuously dry.

Svâmî Narâyanânanda and Nordic journalists

23.4.2001

At five o'clock I arrive at Svâmî Narâyanânanda's *stupa* in the former Mahesh Yogi Ashram. He has two visitors from Norway, a young man and a woman. Both are journalists. They are engaged in making a documentary film about meditation and found their way to the Svâmî by accident. But they also ask many questions to me and I invite them to attend the International Advaita week at the School voor Filosofie's study centre 'Oxerhof' in the autumn of 2001. When the journalists have gone I give some photographs of Shrî Shantânanda Sarasvatî to the Svâmî. He likes them all and looks attentively at every photograph. In the end he keeps one and hands the other ones back to me.

Grace

I put my questions before Svâmî Narâyanânanda. He answers by quoting verses from the Upanishads. To make sure he also looks them up in the texts. He has quite a few old little booklets. 'Grace' is the key. Grace is also 'goodness' but knowledge *jñâna* is necessary. This knowledge will arise through meditation and by 'grace'. He suggests that I should carefully read and study Shvetashvatara Upanishad, verses 3,13 and 3,20. Then I ask Svâmî Narâyanânanda if he would be willing to recite a number of verses from Vivekacûdâmani, as from verse 122 which I would record on my voice recorder.

[Dandi Swami obliges by reciting *'Viveka Chudamani'* - 'The Crest Jewel of Discrimination' and on *'Atman Anatman'*, which refers to the Advaitic thinking, with regards the real v the unreal.]

While I was talking to the journalists Svâmî Narâyanânanda had gone to look for the caretaker in order to help with translation. His English is rather poor and it doesn't really help, but the gesture as such is very considerate. Before taking leave I ask Svâmîjî if I could return the day after tomorrow. Both the Svâmî and the caretaker are very quick to say: *yes, any time, any time.* Their door is wide open for me, that much is clear.

Shvetashvatara Upanishad
25.4.2001

Until three o'clock study, sleeping and meditation. Then I put on my western clothing and my cap in order to go to Svâmî Narâyanânanda. It takes me one hour and a half to get there because of the heat. Twice I had to buy a small bottle of mango juice. The heat is unbearable today. When I finally climb up the hill and when I see the Svâmîjî's *stupa,* I hear that he has gone to the river Ganges to take bath. So I wait for his return.

When he arrives he has a big smile and full of cordiality. We discuss Shvetashvatara Upanishad. For me this text was new but Svâmîjî knows the text by heart. It took me one full day to learn one verse by heart and Shvetashvatara Upanishad has some 110 verses.

Miracles

The Svâmîjî sees no problem to converse with me in a mix of Sanskrit and Hindi. Moreover he talks at great speed and whatever he has to say is almost incomprehensible and abstruse. Still, I listen very carefully and fully concentrated. Then a miracle happens because from time to time I can follow him! Literally. I can hear and understand what he says.

Another neighbour of the *ashram* turns up. 'Holland', 'Holland' the Svâmî tells him pointing at me. Now he hurries inside and I hear him talking in Hindi and saying 'Shantânanda' several times. Then he comes out again with the photograph of Shrî Shântânanda Sarasvatî in his hands, that I had given to him before yesterday. He had fixed a thin iron thread through the punched holes of the plastic cover of the photograph and this meant that he had put up the photograph on the wall of his *stupa.* A great honour, because last time he had shown to me a beautifully framed photograph of Shrî Brahmânanda Sarasvatî (Guru Deva) that had been sent to him by an American lady who had written to him that she had noticed that he had only a black and white photograph of Guru Deva. But he kept this framed photograph in the box as he had received it from the post office. Strangely enough he kept the beautiful colour photograph of Guru Deva in a box and unseen for any one entering his *stupa* whilst he did keep the photograph of Shrî Shântânanda that I had given to him visibly on one of the walls on a thin iron thread. He felt happy because he was happy.

When it is time to leave he beckons me to wait. 'Five minutes' he says. Then he walks away and crosses the large lawn of the *ashram* and returns with a few really scented flowers. They smell of pineapple and are beautiful.

I decided to go by foot for the return journey and once again I had to stop twice to drinks cooled fruit juice. Even when the sun is no longer burning hot, it still is very hot.

The last lap of the road takes me along small smelly alleys full of people, children, pigs, dogs and cows. I sometimes have to push away people to continue my way. Still I feel a sense of unity with them all in an indefinable way. The hustle and bustle of the street is not outside me but especially and above all inside myself. Wherever I look around me, there is no 'around me' nor an 'outside me' but it is all inside me. Once again, a miracle? At ten o'clock in the evening I fall asleep but the walking to and back from the *ashram* take their toll. I wake up several times from an aching pain in my feet.

.... Going back to Svâmî Narâyanânanda's *stupa* my feet do not protest. When I am with Svâmî Narâyanânanda we go through the five *bija mantras* that he had given to me last year. He says that these are potent *mantras*. They were given to him by Shankarâcârya Shrî Shântânanda Sarasvatî. He compares them with atom bombs. They are small and short but have great power. Then I question him further about meditation. It seems to me that the *mantras* are related to *Saguna Brahman* but Shrî Shântânanda always told us to meditate the *Nirguna Brahman*. What about this? The resolute answer is *Nirguna Bram, Nirguna Bram*. It is possible to use these *mantras* for *Saguna Brahman* but one is not supposed to do this. He then quotes from Chandogya Upanishad: *guru vedânta vakya sraddhah*: 'put all your faith in the utterances of the *guru*'.

Shopping with Svâmî Narâyanânanda
29.4.2001

At night there is a thunderstorm and when I wake up at about six o'clock it is still very stuffy and muggy. What does this mean for the rest of the day? At seven o'clock class (Îsha Upanishad) starts. I am still half asleep. At eight o'clock there is a tea break and end of the lecture. Then I have to attend to some laundry and at a quarter to nine I start for going to Svâmî Narâyanânanda. But I meet him half way. He says that he will be back in about one hour. He looks beautiful with his Shankara staff in a silk casing of bright orange colour. It is tied to his shoulder. A majestic appearance.

I move on and now it appears that at the bottom of the hill that gives access to Mahesh Yogi Ashram, the Hari Krishna people have organised some happening. Before this was a waste piece of land on the banks of the river Ganges full of queer types such as peddlers, vagabonds, aged hippies, *saddhus* and quiet hash-smoking people. But since some time a lot of effort has been made to improve the land. There are now fences for shade against the burning sun. When I arrive the first ceremony of the day has just been ended. Everybody stands up. My guess is that there are at least one thousand people who now move about to return home. I sit down and take the time to look at all these people moving along. Colours, forms, sounds everywhere.

After this I move on and climb the hill leading to the *ashram*. I have now some time to move around and to take some pictures of the beautiful panorama that unfolds from the heights above the river Ganges. I see Svâmî Dayananda's Ashram far away at the other side. I sit down on the stone bench in front of Svâmîjî's *stupa* and start meditating. After about a quarter of an hour Svâmî Narâyanânanda returns. There is no greeting. He just goes his own way and it is as if he hadn't noticed me at all. I like this. Simply no unnecessary formalities. When he is ready he comes to sit close to me on his low table where he takes the lotus position. Clearly, the low table is his simple throne.

We talk about meditation for a little while but not too long because the Svâmî has to go out again for some shopping. He takes a large jerry can for kerosene with him. Not so long ago the *ashram* was cut off from water and electricity. The reason for this remains unclear. Are there too many unpaid bills? Has the place been sold by Mahesh Yogi? A few days ago the caretaker had said that a new guesthouse would be built. Svâmî Narâyanânanda tells me that the few families who lived at the other side of the *ashram*, near the caretaker's house, had gone away.

We move together downhill to the small shops. I gave him some money for his purchases. After the necessary refusals and objections he took the money. The first thing he did was buying four large mango fruits. Two of them he gave to me as *prasâdam*. But the vendor refuses to accept any money from Svâmî Narâyanânanda.

We walk together a little further and I notice that the Svâmîjî tries to get rid of me. But I pretend to ignore this. Is it because at the grocer's shop he simply has to wait in the queue? In this shop he is treated without any respect and just like anybody else when he buys kerosene for his lamp. I take some photographs and then take leave of him. Around midday I am back in my room in Svâmî Dayânanda's *ashram*.

Two days later I return to Svâmî Narâyanânanda. It is clear that there is much more activity and livelihood around the *ashram*. The cause of this is the presence of the Hari Krishna movement and the use they make of the refurbished site at the bottom of the hill where the Mahesh Yogi Ashram is situated. This morning there are at least five hundred people present. A few small groups like to take a stroll and walk to the hill and to the *ashram*. They leave Svâmî Narâyanânanda at complete rest and are no disturbance at all but their very presence gives more life to the derelict *ashram*. Svâmî Narâyanânanda tells me that he is seventy years old. It is unclear to me why he suddenly imparts this information to me. Is it his birthday today?

There are dozens of monkeys on the site of the *ashram*. They are much quieter than the baboons. They have a greyish colour with raven-black faces. The baboons are extremely cheeky and Svâmî Narâyanânanda has to chase continuously away with a stick. When I take leave of Svâmîjî I try once again to hand him some money in an envelope. I know that he would not accept so when I take leave I put the envelope under his cushion. He says 'oh', 'oh' and tries to take envelope, but I quickly take leave of him and move out. If he doesn't want to use it, he can always burn it of he can give it to the poor.

....

Excerpts from Rob H. van Dijk's account of his fourth journey to India in April 2002

Meeting again with Svâmî Narâyanânanda
24.4.2002

Having unpacked in our small room in Svâmî Dayânanda's *ashram*, Willeke and I decide to go directly to Svâmî Narâyanânanda. It is one hour's walk. As soon as the wise man in his orange robe notices our arrival he starts to sing and dance of enthusiasm and joy. He moves his head touchingly from left to right in Indian fashion as a sign of approval and appreciation. A joyful reception.

As described earlier Dandî Svâmî Narâyanânanda Sarasvatî as his full name is, lives in very small hut in the form of a *stupa* on a hill alongside the river Ganges and providing a fantastic view on the river. Once it was the flourishing *ashram* of Maharishi Mahesh Yogi and the destination for The Beatles and many other Western celebrities visiting

India in order to meet Maharishi Mahesh Yogi. Svâmîjî leaves us for a moment in order to call the caretaker for translation purposes. Our conversation takes one hour and we take leave of the Svâmî by touching his feet. Then he does something new: he touches us too and blesses us by putting is full hand on our head and shoulders. Wow, that is quite an experience! One feels love, power, strength and warmth. It feels blissful. It is a special token of acceptance. During earlier meetings he kept his hands always at a distance from us.

Second meeting with Svâmî Narâyanânanda
25.4.2002

Willeke gets up at five o'clock and takes a small walk alongside the riverbank. After that she partakes of early morning *puja* at the temple of the Dayânanda *ashram*. I get up at seven and one hour later we walk together to Svâmî Narâyanânanda. The ferryboat has few passengers. It keeps waiting and therefore it takes some time to get across. There is a set timetable on a notice board but nobody takes any notice. Willeke and I say: 'this is a free country' as a practical joke. Strange how we can become quite cheerful with circumstances like this where we would become very impatient when in Holland.

The appointed time is nine o'clock. Because the ferryboat took such a long time, we arrive near the *ashram* at nine thirty. At that moment the Svâmî had just walked down the hill for shopping purposes. When he saw us coming he turned around and walked back to the *ashram* together with us. It is quite a climb but also this year he walks faster than us even at his age!

Yesterday we handed to Svâmîjî a letter from Praan Mahabali and his twelve year old daughter Arti. Praan found our name a month ago through my website www.advaita.nl. We met him and heard many stories of about ten years ago when he was in India in search of spirituality. He met Svâmî Narâyanânanda in Allahabad together with Shrî Shantânanda Sarasvatî, Shankarâcârya. Svâmî Narâyanânanda took the letter of Praan and reads it together with us. It is an occasion to go back to many reminiscences. Svâmî Narâyanânanda has broken all contacts with the *ashram* in Allahabad where Shrî Vasudevânanda Sarasvatî is the present Shankarâcârya. The one person that he still honours is his *guru* Shrî Shântânanda Sarasvatî. Svâmî Narâyanânanda tells us how he travelled over the whole of India by train together with Shrî Shântânanda Sarasvatî and he mentioned twice all the places that they visited. He points them out in the air as if he was standing in the middle. Then I ask Svâmîjî about the Bedford bus that was used by His Holiness. He used the bus regularly by way of comparison for explaining spiritual truths. Svâmîjî confirmed that the bus had been donated by Maharishi Mahesh Yogi to His Holiness.

Third meeting with Svâmî Narâyanânanda
26.4.2002

Willeke gets up at five o'clock. She goes to Ganges River and plunges three times in the cold water as Hindus do in their rituals. After that she returns to Svâmî Dayânanda Ashram for morning puja. Once more we start walking to Svâmîjî but this time driver Rana comes with us. The Svâmî knew about his coming because we had amply told him about him and his impeccable way of looking after us. He is happy to meet Rana.

After our visit Rana would tell us how he was deeply moved by meeting Svâmîjî because it made him happy and because Svâmîjî is a clear example of knowledge, strength, love and simplicity. Qualities he had failed to recognise with most other ochre robed persons.

After the exchange of some personal information with Rana we move on to a discussion about the *Shâstras*, the holy scriptures of Hinduism. Svâmîjî quotes some verses from Katha Upanishad and writes down a verse from Manu-Smriti. Later on he picks up his Bhagavad Gîtâ text and invites me to read verses 38 and 39 from chapter four:

38. There is nothing in the world so purifying as wisdom; and he who is a perfect saint finds that at last in his own self.

39. He who is full of faith attains wisdom and he too who can control his senses. Having attained that wisdom, he shall ere long attain the Supreme Peace.

Acceptance

I have a *mala* and suddenly Svâmîjî asks me what I paid for the *mala*. I do not know because it was given to me by Praan Mahabali. He takes his own *mala* from his shoulders in his hands and says that its cost was more than one hundred rupees, more than two Euro. I see my chance and quickly tell him that mine was two or maybe even three hundred rupees. It was meant as a joke but at the same time it was a chance to suggest exchanging the *malas.* To my surprise he accepts my proposition and this makes me very happy. He understands my desire to seeing him as my *guru* and he puts his *mala* around my neck. I understand that this moment should be fixed on a photograph and I suggest that Willeke will take a photo. Svâmîjî agrees and, once more, he puts the *mala* around my neck. In fact he had to do it twice because the first photograph failed!

Svâmîjî tells Rana that Willeke and I are amongst his most ardent followers. Strange to hear this from the lips of a wise man. He has instructed so many people and shared his knowledge with them. He says that only people who are knowledgeable about diamonds are capable of judging and valuing a rough one. The real beauty of the rough diamond will only come out after the necessary polishing and grinding. Then the diamond becomes really valuable.

As we prepare to take leave from him he rushes inside to get some *prasâdam* for us. I am quick to put some money under his book, knowing that he would never accept money personally. Then he comes out again with three small bags of *prasâdam*. We receive the bags in silence. I bow down to touch his feet and he puts his hand silently on my head by way of blessing.

Fourth meeting
27.4.2002

Together with Rana we arrive at five o'clock precisely at Svâmîjî's *stupa*. I have a question about knowledge, *jñâna*. Yesterday he referred to Bhagavad Gîtâ chapter 4, verses 38 and 39 and understood that *jñâna* is both the means and the goal. Logically speaking this is not possible? I record the elaborate answer on my voice recorder. For Rana it is too difficult to translate since he is not familiar with the subject matter. Several times Svâmîjî refers to passages in Katha Upanishad. Whilst the Svâmî is expounding on this subject a dog comes and lies down near Svâmîjî. He remarks: 'look, this is how *paramâtman* (the true Self) moves in to listen in the form of a dog'.

Meanwhile a strange group of three men comes along. They carry a ghettoblaster with them that blares continuously *Hare Krishna, Hare, Hare* at us. The second man has a stick in his hands. Apparently they are the helpers of the third man who is busy to cover a distance of some 14 miles, which is the distance between two local temples with the length of his body. This means that the third man lies down fully stretched and then he gets up again, but not before the second helper places his stick right between the fingertips of the man to mark the correct place for the man to stand on when getting up and before lying down again for the next step. In this way the complete road is covered by the body length of the devotee. Not one inch can be ignored. We look as they pass-by whilst Svâmîjî enthusiastically encourages the man to persevere. Suddenly I see the connection of the efforts a top sportsman must make to realise his ambitions and the religious efforts of this man. Faith and trust are able to remove mountains and to bring human beings to superhuman efforts.

....

Fifth meeting
28.4.2002

In the afternoon Rana and I will walk again to Svâmîjî. Willeke is not coming with us because she got quite a nasty cut on the sole of her foot when bathing in the river in the morning. Rana overslept and wasn't there and when I was about to move to Svâmî Narâyanânanda some Svâmî from Dayânanda Ashram came to me and started a conversation and in the end he invited me to come to a Vedânta course somewhere in the South of India by Svâmî Dayânanda. With some good will and a little more mental creativity it was possible to see God's helping hand in this hold-up because at that moment Willeke called me and said that Rana had arrived. After the hustle of Rishikesh traffic in the afternoon we arrive at Svâmîjî *stupa*. I hardly dare to look at my watch but in fact we are on time. I am very surprised. We must have caught up with running time. How? I have no idea.

Today the Svâmî is very quiet and silent. There are long pauses of stillness. The topic of conversation is *samskâra*: the personal fate as a result of lingering ambitions and desires that are always around under the surface. They may even go back to previous lives. Svâmî Narâyanânanda says that Willeke's cut in her foot a result may be of *samskâra*. I wish to know more about this and after some pressing Svâmîjî admits that Willeke has been protected against much greater mischief were it not that she was in India and standing in the river Ganges. From the point of view of *samskâra* she was 'in' for much greater mischief but being in India and through the grace of the compassionate Mother Ganga a large 'piece' of *samskâra* is neutralized and silenced by a mere cut of five cm. Small stuff compared to the possible mischief that was waiting for her. Her foot will be healed in four days, he predicts.

Then Svâmîjî takes me by surprise and says that he will come to Dayânanda Ashram the next morning in order to enable Willeke taking leave from him. Rana will collect Svâmîjî at the bridge over the river and take him back again. Well, if Mahomet cannot come to the mountain, the mountain will come to Mahomet!

Sixth meeting
29.4.2002

At eight o'clock in the morning the car that takes Svâmîjî to our apartment in Dayânanda Ashram comes to a halt in front of the apartment. Svâmî Narâyanânanda is a remarkable person with his *dandî* (staff) in an orange coloured silk casing, his grey hair and beard and his tall posture. Even in Dayânanda Ashram where there are many *sannyasins* walking around, he attracts a lot of attention. On our balcony we offer him a chair. Rana goes in to make tea. Svâmîjî doesn't stay long. He enquires after Willeke's foot, tells her that the healing will take four days and that she will be in order again. I walk with him over the *ashram* precinct walking towards the riverfront. From there he can see the Mahesh Yogi *ashram* on the other side of the river. But as soon as he notices the *ashram* temple on his left side, he changes his direction and walks into the temple. Inside he does his prayers in from of the deity and he makes his ritual round through the temple halting at every sculpted image of a deity.

After that he takes a few minutes to enjoy the view over the Ganges River. He sees everything but he does not stay one second longer than necessary.

Then he returns. His elevated state is noticeable and all eyes are fixed on him evoking feelings of awe and respect. I dance around him with my camera. When I ask him to stand next to a tree he willingly obliges. Immediately after that he leaves in the car driven by Rana. The emanation of fine and subtle energy is overwhelming. Here is a man who is master of himself, commanding his surroundings and yet at the same time radiating pure love without 'doing' anything.

Meeting with Shrî Shântânanda Sarasvatî
30.4.2002

Having left Rishikesh for Gangotri, Rob van Dijk finds himself before the gates of the temple of Gangotri, which are still closed. Summer opening in two weeks time.

I stand before the closed gates of the 200-year-old temple. This is the location where Adi Shankara stood some 1200 years ago in order to give instructions for building the temple. It is also the place where Shrî Shântânanda Sarasvatî must have been regularly...

I stand in front of the gate and keep very quiet. Folded hands and closed eyes, surrendering to the stillness. Suddenly all sounds are resounding in one great inner and limitless space without direction and without distance. The darkness of the closed eyes is now transformed into a clear and white light, without any forms. I am aware of all this and slowly it seems as if the light is taking on a form. It is as if I am stepping from darkness into the light and that my eyes need adjusting. The light takes the form of Shrî Shântânanda Sarasvatî. His figure is luminous. He sounds a *mantra* in my mind. His voice is clear and audible. It is one of the five *mantras* as given by Svâmî Narâyanânanda but it sounds quite different: *Om namah Shivâya*. The beautiful and sonorous voice of Shrî Shântânanda leaves a very deep impression behind. Repeating of the *mantra* is now spontaneous. There is no need for *repeating* the *mantra*: it repeats itself and I only listen. The *mantra* is there in all purity and clarity. I stay very still and feelings are kept away. There is total surrender to the situation. Then he beckons me. Time and space, he and me, vanish. I lose consciousness and I do not appreciate that - in fact - I am carried away to a level of consciousness without space and time where I always AM.

Only later I start to understand something of the overwhelming greatness of that experience. I had the intention to ask Svâmî Narâyanânanda to give me a new *mantra* and to establish a teacher-disciple relationship. But I always postponed the question and it was no longer necessary because Svâmîjî had already confirmed in several ways that such a relationship already existed. The fact that I am receiving a new *mantra* in this peculiar way makes me extremely happy. Rana takes the same way the mountain road back to 'the world', a distance of some 100 km. Once in the car I am completely introverted.

* * * * *

Antoine & Dandi Swami Narayananand Saraswati - 7th October 2002

When Eva Bergmann visited Rishikesh in 2002 she sent a message to family and friends:

'Rishikesh is where Maharishi build his first TM academy and this is a place I also wished to visit since many many years, having heard so much about it.

I relished the fresh air and the purity of the atmosphere. I was so happy there that it was hard to move on and I would for sure want to come back there and stay for longer time! The first day I walked up to Maharishi's old ashram, which is abandoned by now, and upon entering there was an old sanyas (recluse) sitting by his little stone hut not far from the entrance. I saw a big picture of Guru Dev (Maharishi's master) on his wall and greeted him with the Jai Guru Dev (all glory to Guru Dev) and he lighted up and we sat and 'talked' a little and he was so beautiful. He said that we are Guru sister and brother since we have the same Guru Dev.

'There are sooooo many sanyasins in India. People who have renounced the world. There were so many in Varanasi, but not all radiate that inner light you would expect from them, and I was told that there are many categories and that many sadhus in fact smoke a lot of marihuana. Not impressive to me!! But the sanyas who are Brahmins live a very pure life, yet I very rarely see someone who impresses me, maybe since I have been so spoiled by being with such long time meditators for so many years.

'But this man was a complete different story. So full of inner bliss and simplicity. He showed me his little stone hut room and his very few belongings. There is no electricity or running water there anymore, and whereas he could live with the group now in Uttar Kashi further north, he said it is too cold, and I can say it was cold enough at night in Rishikesh in December (and in January I heard that the cold became even worse than normal!!). He said he only had one blanket and that he bathes in Ganges every morning. Brrrrrr.

'He showed me and the lady I was walking with around the whole place and recently there had been elephants doing damage to the trees! Their remains left no doubt that it was recent history.

'Everything is falling apart but it is still touching to see Maharishi's house and all the facilities, which Maharishi himself helped to form.

'As you can imagine knowing me, then I just wanted to help making this sanyas more comfortable. So I was thinking of all the things I wanted to buy him and the next day, when I finally had time to go out and buy things I ran into him right outside where I lived and with some translation help I could ask if he would like some new clothes? So in the end we went shopping together for him, and this was infinitely better that me doing it, because I had already looked the day before, but then I could ask if he liked those things, but he just accepted very simple things like another orange wool blanket (sanyas wear orange) and we went to Rishikesh to get a new dhoti (the cloth men wrap around them) and some socks! I kept asking if he did not want new shoes, fruits, some holy books or anything, and he was so inspiring in his simple living. No, he only wanted what was necessary. Anyone else would have been moved by greed, but this was absolutely absent in him. Just walking next to him was a great pleasure for me, because I love to move with consciousness. So you can understand that it was a most precious experience to me. I was a little worried I had bothered him with asking if he wanted this or that, but later someone wanted to walk up to Maharishi's ashram, and I went to meditate there, and we met shortly again and his pointed to his socks, and said very good!! And I brought a few pieces fruit for his worship. So all this warms my heart!

The first day I visited he also showed that he was interested in one thing. I thought he meant a coat, but it turned out to be a sleeping bag. He had me write the name in English for him. So since I was going south I thought I would not need my sleeping bag as much as he would, so I gave him mine plus my thermal mat. After that when I met him, he said he could sleep just with a loin cloth. So knowing that he is 72 years old, I felt it was time to be comfortable! Before leaving I found out that the receptionist at the ashram I was staying at grew up with Maharishi, so we agreed that if my guru brother ever needs anything, he should contact me.'

– 10 –

Premanand Paul Mason sits with Dandi Swami Narayananand Saraswati - late 2002

'I notice that Dandi Swami wears a ring on one of his fingers, and I wonder if at one time he has been married. He laughs at the suggestion, and tells me; 'For health, health ring is for'.

'When I visit Dandi Swami with Norwegian friend Oddbull Indramurti, he offers to take us for a walk around the *ashram*. It is late afternoon and there is little light to guide our way, but all the while we hear the steady, tap, tap, tap of Dandi Swami's *danda* stick hitting the ground. We follow behind him, and I hear him chuckling to himself. It becomes suddenly cold, and very dark, in fact it is hard to make out anything in the sudden darkness. However, I hear the steady tap, tap, tap of the *danda* striking hard ground. The image of the blind old Shaolin monk, Master Po, from David Carradine's Kung Fu television series comes to mind. Could it be that Dandi Swami is testing me, as the blind old monk had tested 'Grasshopper' Kwai Chang Caine, the novice? I continue, somewhat concerned that I will trip or fall, as I sense my feet catching on uneven ground, and now I am walking through a shallow pool of water. When all of a sudden, the way becomes better lit - a shaft of daylight seems to light up the way ahead a little. And then I get it, Dandi Swami brought us through a secret entrance and we are walking underground to where the derelict lecture hall still stands. Now, in the light, we all three of us stand about laughing. If this is a test, it might also be Dandi Swami's way of a having a lark?'

* * * * *

Excerpts from Rob H. van Dijk's account of his fifth journey to India in May 2003

A year later, back in Rishikesh
9.5.2003

Next day we go to the Dayânanda *ashram*, but a number of groups are staying at the *ashram*, which is fully booked. But the *ashram* office always keeps a few rooms free in case of an emergency. So they give us one of these three-bed rooms.

That same afternoon we go to Svâmî Narâyanânanda. One hour's walk. He is doing his midday nap and we wait until he gets up. The meeting again is very affectionate. I give him the self-made gifts of my mother and of Willeke. My mother made a lily flower in clip art and it gives great pleasure to Svâmîjî. Svâmîjî showed us the photographs of Willeke and me that were given to him by my son Erik about a month ago. In fact he took them from Eric and kept them.

In view of the sickness of Erik, Svâmî Narâyanânanda quoted some verses from Bhagavad Gîtâ: Ch 6,17; 13,17; and 7,4-5. On my return to Dayânanda Ashram I buy the text of Bhagavad Gîtâ with the commentary of Svâmî Sivânanda. That is always a good investment.

Bh.G. VI,17:

'But for him who regulates his food and recreation, who is balanced in action, in sleep and in waking it shall dispel all unhappiness.'

Bh.G. XIII,17:

'It is the light of lights, beyond the reach of darkness, the wisdom, the only thing that is worth knowing or that wisdom can teach; the presence in the hearts of all.'

Bh.G. VII,4-5:

'Earth, water, fire, air, ether, mind, intellect and personality; this is the eightfold division of my manifested nature.

This is my inferior nature; but distinct from this, O Valiant One! know thou that my superior nature is the very life which sustains the universe.'

My *guru* sends me away
10.5.2003

The Svâmî tells me: 'there is nothing to seek for you with me any more'. 'Why don't you go to Badrinath and Joshimath? There is the seat of our *Gurudeva*, Shrî Shântânanda Sarasvatî and his successor, Shrî Vasudevânanda'. By addressing Shrî Shântânanda Sarasvatî as *gurudeva* he refers to him as his teacher and as the source of the knowledge that has come to him (Svâmî Narâyanânanda). Erik observed: 'well, Rob, I just wanted to suggest that there is little to look for here, because you are already saying the same things as the Svâmî.'

I know that it is not uncommon that *gurus* send their disciples away when they find that the learning period is over. If they would not do that the teacher-disciple relationship could easily turn into negative emotions rather than remaining positive. But that this would happen so quickly, was quite unexpected.

To Joshimath and the throne of Shrî Shântânanda
12.5.2003

On 11th May Rob, Erik and Rana travel by car to Joshimath. They first arrive at the Svarûpânanda ashram and the following day they go to the original ashram of Shrî Shântânanda Sarasvatî and now of His Holiness Shrî Vasudevânanda Sarasvatî.

The next day we walk a little further uphill just behind the holy 'Shankara tree'. There is a gap in high wall around a garden with a small gate. We enter into a large garden through the gate and notice at the end of the garden a large wooden building with two storeys. It is an old building and on the first floor there is a beautiful and large wooden veranda. This is the original *ashram*, which is now occupied by Shrî Vasudevânanda. His name is marked above the door. Is it not strange that all the people from the building below, which belongs to Shrî Svarûpânanda, completely ignore the existence of this building and the *ashram* itself? They even deny its very existence! Of course they know of this building and of its purpose. Both buildings and gardens are adjacent to each other with Shankara's tree as the point of division. The older *ashram* stands above the newer one.

A little later I tell this story to an older Sannyâsin who acts as caretaker for the Vasudevânanda *ashram*. He takes us to the audience room in the building with throne of HH Shrî Shântânanda Sarasvatî. On the walls are pictures of the three preceding Shankarâcaryas: Shri Brahmânanda Sarasvatî, Shri Shântânanda Sarasvatî and Shrî Vishnudevânanda Sarasvatî. On the throne itself there is a picture of Shrî Vasudevânanda Sarasvatî. All this is totally ignored by the people of the *ashram* below. They are consciously and with a purpose telling lies and deny the existence of the old and traditional *ashram.*

When I share my understanding with the caretaker-sannyâsin and vent my surprise that sannyâsins/monks can tell straight lies he simply smiles and says: 'that is their duty'. They are meant to do this. For him this is the end of the story. No disappointment or any form of anger in his voice. He stays completely calm. Erik and I are deeply moved by this answer. This moment we shall not forget. We decide to meditate in the audience hall with the photographs of the Shankarâcâryas. There is a peaceful stillness. We are taken up in this stillness. It is marvelous to feel so relaxed.

Meeting on the veranda

After meditation we have a conversation with a few very kind and most friendly *sannyâsins.* Once more time is a very relative phenomenon. No worries, no hurry no distrust. How simple and happy life can be!

We are sitting with the five of us on the floor of the old veranda. We enjoy a beautiful view on the snow-covered mountaintops of the Himalayas. We are sitting in the most peaceful surroundings imaginable. Every now and then something is said and then there is the stillness again. This continues without any stress or sense of hurry arising. There is no need to keep the conversation going. (What a strange habit to keep the conversation going!). Here is communication without words. Here is peace and happiness. That is what is communicated.

Back with Svâmî Narâyanânanda
14.5.2003

At ten o'clock in the morning we return to Svâmîjî's little *stupa.* Rana gives a short description of our journey and how we were confronted with two rival *ashrams* in Joshimath. The Svâmî recognises the story and tells us his own version. Circumstances in Joshimath got so heated that there was a risk of people going at each other's throat and killing someone. This prompts Shrî Shântânanda to step down as Shankarâcârya. He wanted to have Svâmî Narâyanânanda is his successor, now 23 years ago, but the Svâmî declined. He preferred to live in solitude rather than in such warlike circumstances. Last year he told us that his *guru* Shrî Shântânanda Sarasvatî had advised him to live in solitude and that he had appointed Shrî Vishnudevânanda Sarasvatî as his successor.

In the evening it becomes clear to me that this is my last trip to India. From a physical point of view I live in a dream and I can go anywhere in the world without the need of taking an airplane or any other means of transport. From a subtle point of view I live in the Light of lights. Bh.G. XIII,17:

It is the light of lights, beyond the reach of darkness, the wisdom, the only thing that is worth knowing or that wisdom can teach; the presence in the hearts of all.

This waking dreamstate is for me no longer attractive. Neither the dreaming state in sleep.

I have the distinct impression that a lot of ballast of the past year has been churned up and dissolved. This has not been a pleasant experience but thanks are to Shiva: *Om namah Shivâya.*

* * * * *

In September 2003, in a global news conference, broadcast by satellite hookup, Maharishi Mahesh Yogi shares his views about government:

"No system of administration – monarchy, democracy, dictatorship – is ideal because no system can prevent problems for the people,"

"Our slogan is 'damn democracy' because there is no democracy in the world today. It is a bloody, destructive dictatorship in the name of democracy."

* * * * *

Dandi Swami Narayananand Saraswati
'Gurus' - BBC3 television - 2003

When the Texan model and former wife of Mick Jagger, Jerry Hall, visits the ruins of Maharishi Mahesh Yogi's former *ashram*, she interviews Dandi Swami Narayananand Saraswati in connection with her documentary series entitled 'Gurus' in 2003. Clearly she hopes to talk to him about The Beatles' famous visit to Rishikesh, however, in 1968 Dandi Swami was elsewhere, in the service of Shankaracharya Shantanand Saraswati.

'Mataji', the wealthy young Indian woman who arrived in Los Angeles in 1959 to serve Maharishi, is now an old lady. She is known both as Sitadevi Mata Ji and Sita Agrawal and lives at Gita Bhavan, in Swargashram, quite near Maharishi Ashram. Apparently, she has a pair of sandals that used to be worn by Swami Brahmanand Saraswati, which she does *puja* to. Also, she has an original copy of *'Amrit Kana'*, an early book of Guru Dev quotations, compiled by Maharishi, when he was known as Brahmachari Mahesh.

* * * * *

The Natural Law Party, the Maharishi's political wing, announces its disbandment in 2003 in the UK, and in 2004 the USA also disbanded most of their operations, which had even included fielding a Presidential candidate.

* * * * *

Writer/ researcher Dana Sawyer with Dandi Swami - 24th May 2005

– 11 –

By 2006, Dandi Swami has moved from his *kutir* at 'The Beatles Ashram' having been offered alternate accommodation by the Swargashram Trust. He moves into a modest dwelling place quite near the shore of the River Ganges, between the villages of Swargashram and Lakshman Jhula, and through word of mouth, well wishers would seek him out.

Here are some delightful photos taken by a Dutch couple, visiting Dandi Swami at his hermitage, in 2006.

Dandi Swami Narayananand Saraswati - 4th April 2006

Dutch couple sit with Dandi Swami ji - 5th April 2006

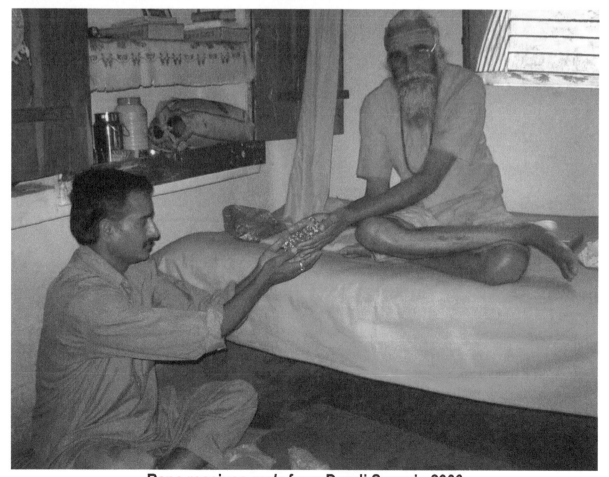

Rana receives *mala* from Dandi Swami - 2006

Dandi Swami Narayananand Saraswati - 20th April 2006

* * * * *

– 12 –

kutir 54, Swargashram Trust, Rishikesh 31st December 2006

Bjarne Hansen recalls arriving in Rishikesh and trying to locate Dandi Swami: -

'The time record on this photo shows it was shot on New Years Eve 31. Dec 2006, the day before we actually met him.

I recall we looked for him on the 31st. on the banks of Ganga showing your photo to many of the locals. Finally an old man told us: "You will see him, not today …. Tomorrow" and this dog literally walked us to his place. Sounds a little mystic, but this is how we found the place, and next day the same dog waited at the gate. Rishikesh is magical mystery tour.

The photo is of the dog that finally showed us the way to the Cotier. Yes, it is a sweet story that I carry in my heart, some of these semi-wild dogs in India are amazing, heard so many stories of them when we trekked in Himachal province. Need to go for now, but so good to get back all those precious memories. Thank You!

"My wife Vibeke and I spent New Year's day of 2007 with Dandiswami in Rishikesh - puja, meditation, spiritual jokes and laughter.... That was when the short video of him was shot. Now, his English was not good but anyhow, we were able to communicate.

Me and My wife Vibeke spent maybe 1 or 2 hours with him. I will try to recollect the subjects covered with Vibeke in a few days and also see if I can find some more photos.

Bjarne Hansen & Dandi Swami ji - 1st January 2007

We will try to go through our memories in a while. He asked to MMY [Maharishi Mahesh Yogi] and his health and also talked on meditation, Bhagavadgita, personal God versus Advaita. And time. Vibeke has a good memory so I will come back in a few days when we have been seating our storehouse of memories.

Dandiswami insisted I knew someone named Eva in Denmark, and I had to reply to him; 'No.... there are so many Evas in Denmark, no chance,....' But he insisted and gave me a telephone number.

Now when we returned from India I made the call and found I knew Eva, indeed she had been my neighbour for a short while in 1982, in Sweden, .. & I had not talked to her for decades.

It's a small world and Rishikesh is magic, thanks to Souls like Dandiswami, since thousands of years ...."

"Dandiswami was very fond of Eva Bergmann as she helped him in small ways such as buying warm clothes etc."

* * * * *

Dandi Swami Narayananand Saraswati
photo: Gunnar Muhlmann

photo: Gunnar Muhlmann

In October 2007 a young couple meet with Dandi Swami and take some beautiful photographs of their visit.

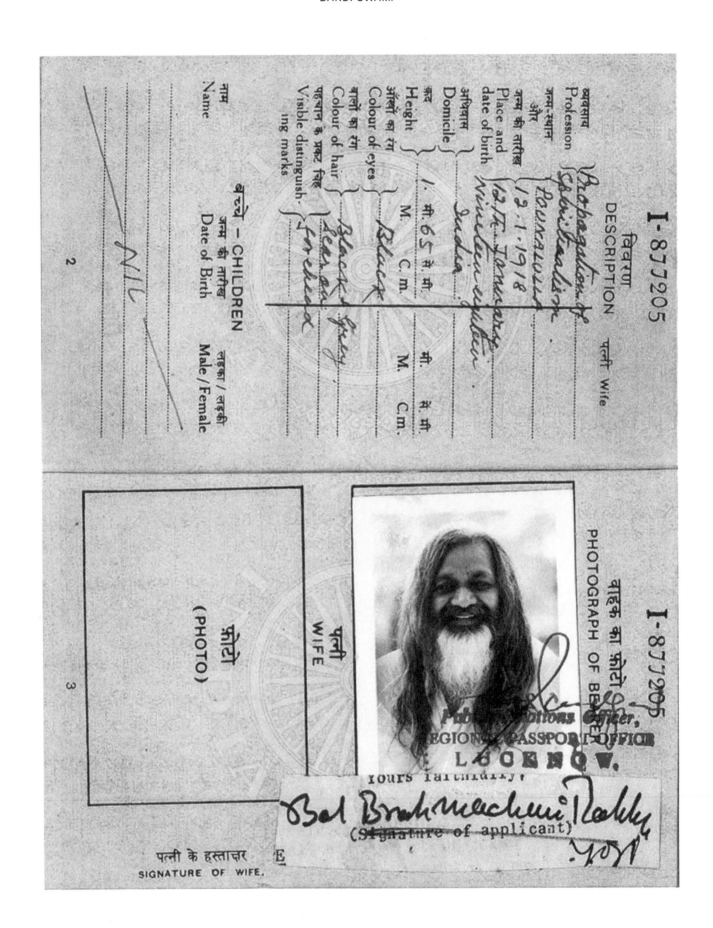

– 13 –

It is reported, that on 5th February 2008, Maharishi Mahesh Yogi, famous for his spreading of Transcendental Meditation, has died in Vlodrop, Holland.

A week later, on 12th February 2008, his body is cremated by the Ganges, at Allahabad, India.

It is announced that Maharishi named Tony Abu Nader, the Lebanese neuro-scientist, as his successor. He is crowned and is to be addressed as Maharaja Adhiraj Raja Ram – *'adhiraj'* meaning sovereign

* * * * *

In May 2009 a three-volume set of books; *'The Life and Teachings of Shankaracharya Swami Brahmanand Saraswati, Shankaracharya of Jyotir Math (1941-1963)'*, is published by Premanand, in the UK. The books are translations of out-of-print Hindi publications, previously published by the *guru's* own *ashram*, now translated by Premanand Paul Mason, who has also added additional material. The work is dedicated to Dandi Swami Narayananand Saraswati.

In 2008, David Sieveking, a young filmmaker from Germany, contacts Paul Mason, and confides that he is planning to make a documentary about his experiences with Transcendental Meditation and the organisation that promotes it. Paul suggests several people that David might interview, in Europe, the USA and India, including giving David details of how he might contact Dandi Swami Narayananand Saraswati.

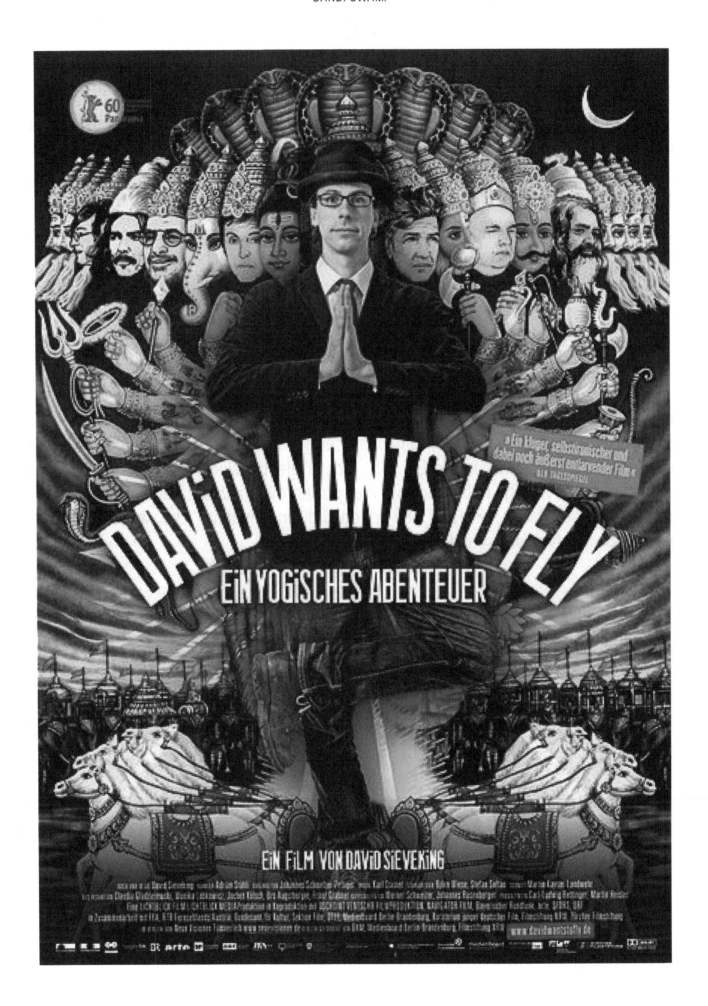

– 14 –

Shankaracharya Swami Swaroopanand Saraswati

Before visiting Dandi Swami in Rishikesh, David Sieveking decides to visit Swami Swaroopanand Saraswati, the eighty-five year old claims to be both Shankaracharya of Dwaraka, and also Shankaracharya of Jyotirmath. So, on 22nd May 2009, David meets with Swami Swaroopanand at his *ashram* at Jabalpur, and hears the eighty-five year olds' recollections of events leading up to Swami Brahmanand's death, and his explanation as to how the dispute over the Shankaracharya of Jyotirmath's succession came about.

David is helped by followers of Swami Swaroopanand, who translate his questions into Hindi and translate the *swami's* answers into English. Sometimes the *brahmacharis* just give their interpretations as to what their teacher is saying: -

Swami Swaroopanand recalls: - "Gurudev had reached Kashi to abandon his body and take leave for his heavenly abode. When we learnt of it, all of us rushed to Kashi to take his final blessings. His health was deteriorating and people were wondering as to who would succeed him. At that time Mahesh asked him to go with him to Kolkatta where there is better medication. We all opposed this move as any travelling would worsen the situation but an astrologer was brought in, who predicted that he would live till he would be 125 years, and hence he should travel. As soon as he reached Kolkatta, he dies within four days!

"Now Sita Saraf was in Kolkatta when Gurudev passed away and she along with Mahesh played out a drama claiming that they asked Gurudev to accept their lives but Gurudev refused and passed away. It was also spread far and wide that when Gurudev's soul was leaving his body, Mahesh Yogi's soul was also exiting but Gurudev pushed his soul back because Mahesh had to complete Gurudev's incomplete work for which he had to go abroad!!!

"He was again brought back to Kaashi where his final rites were done.

"After Gurudev's demise he spread the news that there is a Will made by Gurudev on his name and that claims him to be Gurudev's disciple...

"The will named four people- Shantanand, Dwarka Prasad Shastri, Vishnudevanand and Parmanand. Now when the Will was opened for reading it turned out that Shantanand did not understand Sanskrit, he used to work for Geeta press on the salary of 14 rupees per month and thus was not capable enough, Dwarkaprasad Shastri was a married man with family, Vishnudevanand was not educated enough and Parmanand's big toe on the right leg was amputed and someone who is disabled is not given sannyas, thus he was nullified. So the four were rejected and Swami Krishnabodhashramji was made Shankaracharya, but Mahesh Yogi instigated Shantanand to fight the court case. He was given a car and money and all other assistance and help.

"Also, as per the will that was revealed, it stated clearly that the order of succession was to be Shantanand, Dwarkaprasad Shastri, Vishnudevanand and Parmanand. However all of them passed away in exactly the reverse order! If Gurudev who has the far sight to foresee such events had written the will how could they all pass away in exactly the reverse order??

"Therefore... he was a 'siddha mahatma', why was this in reverse order?"

"So for this reason this is it, that his name was put to these.

"Thus it was a Will that was tampered by Mahesh Yogi and his associates."

According to Swaroopanand, Maharishi Mahesh Yogi, is neither a 'Maharishi' (a great rishi, or sage) nor a 'Yogi' (one who has mastered yoga): -

"I was the disciple of Gurudev and had taken into his fold through a ceremony called Dand Sanyaas which Mahesh Yogi could not get done as he was not a Brahman. Also Mahesh was his secretary and he was not Gurudev's disciple in any way but was a part of the administrative staff."

"So far as I know he did not know anything about yoga so I have no idea how he became Yogi.

"But he was very smart and shrewd. He was responsible for the controversy over Shankaracharyas here in Jyotirmath. He wanted to put up here a Shankaracharya who would listen to him. That was his motive behind dividing the Jyotirmath..

"He divided the Jyotirmath into two Shankaracharyas so that the other Shankaracharya does not speak anything negative about him. That was his intention behind dividing.

"When Sita Saraf fell ill, Maharishi took her to south India for treatment and with her money later flew to Singapore. In south there was a Maharishi Ramana from where Mahesh Yogiji picked up the title of 'Maharishi' for himself. Generally this is a title that is given by the people but in his case he picked it up himself.

"The Shankaracharya that he appointed was illiterate. Mahesh Yogi gave him his car to use and would pay him 30,000 per month. He would in turn call him 'Maharishi' and stand up when Mahesh Yogi entered the room.

"After Gurudev's death he left India, there was a lady called Sita Saraf who gave him money and he left for Singapore from where he left for America and started teaching Bhavateet Yoga there.

"It is that.... Gurudev was a Mahatma and we must spread his word, so in that regard we will praise Mahesh Yogi for spreading Gurudev's name amongst the people."

Swami Brahmanand Saraswati 1871-1953

Swami Shantanand Saraswati 1913-1997

Dandi Swami Narayananand Saraswati - 1st June 2009
photo: Adrian Stähli

David Sieveking goes to Rishikesh, with his film crew, to meet with Dandi Swami Narayananand, and interviews him at the front of his *kutir*. On June 1st 2009 David asks some questions in English to Dandi Swami, which are then translated into Hindi. However, since Dandi Swami is 'in silence' he writes his answers in Hindi, so David's translator then conveys these back into English, as best he can.

David Sieveking asks Dandi Swami Narayananand Saraswati a few questions

David: - *Dandi Swami Narayanand, it's nice to have the opportunity to meet you. I heard that you were once the disciple of Brahmanand Saraswati, Guru Dev, and you also got to know Maharishi Mahesh Yogi in that time, in service of Brahmanand Saraswati. Is this correct?*

Such a beautiful handwriting, that…

Translator: - *He says; he was.. err... Brahmanandji Saraswati... At the time of Brahmanandji Saraswati he not lived with him. He knew him, and while coming or going he used to have 'darshan' of him but he never stayed as a disciple with Brahmanand Saraswati.*

David: - *Okay, but is there, is there, he... what is his feeling towards Brahmanand Saraswati, what does he think of him?*

Translator: - *He very highly regards Gurudevji, and he says his whole life was like the idol of, the meditation, and he was like a god... that's what he feels.*

David laughs and asks: - *Can he show us the, the... does he have a picture, of that time, of Guru Dev for instance...?*

Translator: -

David: - *Yes? Can he show us? Ask him if he has another picture of that time, of himself or something.*

Translator: - *Jai Gurudev.*

David: - *Very nice pictures, can I see?*

Translator: *Shantanand Ji*

David: - *Shankaracharya Swami Shantanand. He stayed in his service for a while? Brahmachari? Shankaracharya Ashram, ha, ha.*

Translator: - *Shantanandji Saraswati, from him only he got this 'diksha', the ceremony of 'sannyas'...*

David: - *Okay, he became a 'sannyasin'...*

Translator: - *Through Shantanandji Saraswati, and this name - Dandi Swami Narayananand Saraswati - is given by Shantanandji to him.*

David: - *Ah, okay, beautiful! And, and, I have one... He seems to be such a comfortable happy person. Totally at ease. What is his, what is his secret, for his happiness?*

Translator: - *These are the four secrets - 'guru kripa', it is because of .. ummm.. guru's teachings, 'guru's blessings'. 'kripa' means blessings you can say. So, guru's blessings, secondly; sadhana, bhajan and dhyaan, like meditation, and bhajan is praising god, that is a different kind of a word, 'bhajan', bhajan is usually like, um, praising of gods. So, 'sadhana'....*

David: - *Through meditation...?*

Translator: - *Through meditation!*

Translator: - *Okay, direct, influence of that meditation, direct influ .. ah, ha, has and his 'brahmachari jeevan'.*

David: - *What is 'brahmachari jeevan'?*

Translator: - *'brahmachari' means, oh I don't ...*

Dandi Swami: - *nn, nnn, nnn...*

Translator: - *They don't indulge into....*

Dandi Swami: - *nna, nn...*

Translator: - *No marriage!*

David: - *Ah, okay! (laughs) You think it's better?*

Dandi Swami: - *nna, nn...*

David: - *You think it's better? Better don't have, don't have a girlfriend? (laughs) Ha, ha, ha, ha!*

Translator: - *And 'ekaant vaas', is, its staying alone*

David: - *Staying alone. Huh!*

Translator: - *This is all due to the, and med... Might be also because he is staying and meditating in, near the, around Himalayas, so getting influence on his happiness, and his peaceful life. He looks very content.*

David: - *Yes, yes, he does. And, and, did he never, he never was in love with a woman, in his life?*

Translator asks the question to Dandi Swami.

David seems to get the answer by non-verbal means: - *Never! Okay. (laughs) But what is his...?* (David is still laughing)

Translator: - *Connection to the god always, he is saying.*

David: - *No disturbance?* (more laughter) *What is advice for me? I am a, I'm not a, very advanced meditator. I'm very much in this material world still, and I love women, I want to have a family. But I also am looking for some connection, to something higher. What is his advice, what shall I try to do?*

I'm also looking for the happiness he radiates.

(Several minutes roll by before the translator gives Dandi Swami's response.)

Translator: - *Anything is, it's about; 'sugandha' is a good smell, 'sugandha', so, a good smell everybody likes.. Like that, yuh, like that, a person whose, whose atma, whose soul is great, pure, if you sit below, aside him, if you sit alongside him, in the same way, you'll feel peace, like you.., like the smell, like that.*

David: - *So he advised me to get near people with a great aatma?*

Translator: - *Yuh.*

Translator: - *This is for him, he said. You said, you asked how he managed. The soul is so pure; the soul is so strong....*

David: - *Can you find the meaning?*

Translator: - *... around him..... No marriage. No friend. Meditation. If you want to make your life beautiful, so read Bhagavad Gita, and then...*

David: - *I have, I have already.*

Translator: - *Read it again ... then you'll find peace in your life. Okay, he says if you want to be in the materialistic world then you have get married and have childrens, but then read Bhagavad Gita, they you will find peace in your life.*

David: - *But he is saying the best would be not to marry and renounce, and to.. to meditate?*

Translator: - *Yuh.*

David: - *But he also says it is possible to have a family and raise kids and but it's important to read the Bhagavad Gita?*

Translator: - *Yuh..... Meditation also.*

David, after waiting for Dandi Swami to write his answer: - *Later on, we can publish a book with all his... sentences....*

Translator: - *What he is saying is, one of his disciple is from Holland.*

David: - *Holland?*

Translator: - *Holland, Holland. Ahh, he has come here many times, and on the Internet he has given on the... achha, about him, and Shantanandji.*

David: - *Ah that's good!*

Translator: - *About his life also, there is an introduction, on Internet, and after reading the Gita both of them, their life has changed. And both of them are doctors.*

David: - *Okay.*

Translator: - *They are a couple and both of them are doctors, but after reading the Gita their life has changed.*

David: - *Okay.*

Dandi Swami: - (laughing)

David: - *Okay.*

Dandi Swami: - (still laughing)

David: - *I have read the Gita and I like it very much but it is, there some things that are hard to understand for me, for instance how can I ever be free of desire, for anything, for instance, also to meditate is a desire, to know I am meditating to be happy person. So how can I ever be free of desire..? And, this is my first question.*

Translator: - *He is saying; you will not get it so fast.*

David: - *Ahem.*

Translator: - *Slowly and steadily when you try and learn it, then only you will get it. The process is very slow.*

David: - *You get, then you get free from desire, any desire, any kind of desire, or what, what do you mean?*

Translator: - *No, no, no.* (confused voices) *To understand the meaning, the gist of it, it's a very slow process*

David: - *It's a lifelong process, probably?*

Translator: - *Yes, so you have to study it, very hard and hard. Then you'll get something from it.*

David: - *And, but how, eh one.... There we go... But one thing that is very important in Hinduism, and I like it very much. is ahimsa, No Violence, ahimsa, but in the Bhagavad Gita, it's a war story, and at the end Krishna tells Arjuna; 'Kill'. 'Go into the war, do your duty' This I don't understand, it doesn't get together, it is a contradiction.*

Why does, why does Krishna, so powerful, the god, let this happen? This violence, this war, and the suffering.. Why does Krishna err, not, not change this?

Translator: - (starts singing) *'... the answer you get but.. '* (and David laughs..) *Okay, okay, okay...* (Indistinct chatter between them)

David: - *Because I don't understand, Krishna is so powerful, and why does he let so much evil and suffering happen, and that? Why doesn't he make it a peaceful life, heaven on earth? Why doesn't Krishna do that?*

It is the same answer.

Translator: - (muffled for a few sentences). *You have to find your own answers.*

David: - *Has he said that?*

Translator: - *No, no.*

David: - *Why isn't there...? Can you ask him why is there violence and, suffering and evil in the world if there is a creating power like God?*

Translator: - *What he is saying; If you feel the 'I am doing this', then it is not like that.*

David: - *Okay.*

Translator: - *To make you do that is someone else.*

David: - *Like destiny...like fate.*

Translator: - *And, to understand him, you have to meditate.*

David: - *Mmm.*

Translator: - *Understand, who he is.*

David: - *Who's running... the creator.. uh? Okay. So I have to meditate about this, yeh?*

Translator: - *Yes.*

David: - *Can you tell him, I learned the Transcendental Meditation technique and I came to know Maharishi. And, but, I have a little, em, problem, because they, in that kind of meditation, you never, you're not supposed to think about the creator or God or anything. And what does he think about Maharishi's teachings?*

And ask him... okay that we, will...

- Oh look, pyrotechnics... Okay, that's great.... Yes, we just wait for ten minutes and then finished and then we talk about it. -

Translator: - *He'll not give an answer about Maharishi ji. Somewhere you have to take 'aashraya', 'aashraya' means, shelter, somewhere you have to take shelter. Without support, no one can survive. By earth's support the life alone goes on.*

David: - *Is he referring to the meditation? What kind of meditation he is following? Is it similar to the, what Maharishi is teaching? Is it a mantra meditation, no?*

Translator: - *Err, Maharshi..* (then speaks in mumbled Hindi) *He is saying; whatever he was teaching was okay.*

David: - *Yuh! One more question... Can you believe that yogic flying is possible?* (laughing) *Uh, just hopping! That's good, okay, okay.* (laughter) *Thank you. The last question is what, how is he meditating. Himself? He doesn't want to say! Okay, okay.. Okay, it's secret, secret.*

Okay, okay, em, I am going to, em, in the next days, I am going to the Himalaya for to see, to meditate on, on nature, yes? Yes, yes, yup. It's coming already, yeh. And what does his, does he have any advice for me, where to go? Erm, I'm going, I want to go to Gangotri, em, what shall I, can he give me advice, what I shall I do there?

No advice! Hmm (laughing). *Ha, ha, hmm, ha. I have to find out myself, yuh? Yep. Okay, em shukriya, thank you very much. What's... wonderful, yeah! Em, tell him erm, I'm in contact with the, Paul Mason, who visited him.*

Translator: - *Okay.*

David: - *And he asked me if I could give him, erm, err, record of our conversation, and, if he allows to. Then I will also give him a record of the conversation, if we have time.. Can you ask him if it's fine?*

Translator: - *Paul, give it to Paul Mason.*

David: - *Paul Mason, remember, remember, ask him if he remembers Paul Mason, when you mention...*

Translator: - *Ask Paul...* (And there the recording ends!!)

* * * * *

– 16 –

**Dandi Swami Narayananand Saraswati - 11th November 2009
holding print of a photo taken three years earlier**
photo: Randy Anand

Randy Anand meets with Dandi Swami in November 2009: *"I had visited Rishikesh over 25 times over the last years and had heard and read about Dandi Swami but somehow never met him even though I had been inside Shankaracharya Nagar ashram even when Dandi Swami was living there.*

During one of my trips to Rishikesh I asked a friend who lives in Rishikesh and knew of Dandi Swami if he would take me to him and act as translator. He was not able to go with me, but directed me as to the general area where Swamiji was living. When I arrived to the area, I asked a local sannyasi if he knew where Swami Narayananda's place was.

He said "You mean Dandi Swami?" and I immediately realized that the locals knew him by that name, and I said, "Yes, Dandi Swami".

He pointed to a small cottage and I walked there.

Upon arriving Swamiji saw me and I said "Jai Guru Dev". He seemed very happy to see me and motioned for me to come unto to his veranda while he got a plastic chair for me to sit on.

He pointed to his mouth and shook his head and I realized that he was not speaking.

So I said "mauna?", which in the Hindi language means silence, and he shook his head yes and giggled. He then pulled out a newspaper that was in English that had a big article about the upcoming Kumbha Mela, which was a few months later. At first, I did not understand why he was showing me the article and then I realized that he was saying that he would remain in silence until the Kumbha Mela began, which was not for another two months or so.

As I now knew he was in silence, and I didn't know how much English he understood, I tried to communicate as simply as possible by pointing to myself and said "Dhyan-Maharishi Mahesh Yogi". He understood and stood up and went into his cottage and pulled out his photos of Guru Dev and Swami Shantanand. He proudly held them up and I pointed to each photo and said their names, and he giggled again. It was a very sweet sound. I took a photo as he held his pictures and I pointed to Shantanand's image and asked him "Guruji?" as if to ask, "Is Shantanand your guru?" He shook his head yes.

Then we sat for a little while and I pulled out of my bag photos I had printed from the Internet of him. He really enjoyed that and seemed to think it was very funny that I had those photos, and he giggled for quite a while.

As there was not much to say at that point, I simply said "Dhyan?", to ask him if we could meditate together for a while. He responded by pulling his legs up into lotus position. I got comfortable and we meditated for about 15 minutes.

Then it was time to go, so I bowed and said "Thank you" in Hindi and "Jai Guru Dev".

He waved as I walked away and I felt very happy that I had finally been able to meet him.

I tried to go back and see him on a later trip [August 2011] and went to his cottage, but another swami was there and informed me that Dandi Swami had left his body several months previously. I was sad that he was no longer with us, but was thankful for that one special time with him.

I have been lucky enough to meet many saints on my various trips to India and being around them is always a wonderful experience. But I can say that he radiated a purity, a simplicity, and a level of happiness that was quite unique."

Dandi Swami Narayananand Saraswati - 11th November 2009
photo: Randy Anand

Email to "Paul Mason" <premanandpaul@yahoo.co.uk>
Date: Thursday, 4 November 2010, 10:31:10

I will try to find Swami Narayananda in Rishikesh again and if I see him I will let you know how he is doing. He really enjoyed those photos that you sent me when I met with him last year.

Randy

* * * * *

Email to "Paul Mason" <premanandpaul@yahoo.co.uk>
Date: Tuesday, 17 April, 2012, 6:11

Paul,

I went to Kutir 54 yesterday. Met a sadhu living there. Said that Narayanand had lived there. But he passed away three years ago.

Steve Krivit

* * * * *

It is said that Dandi Swami Narayananand Saraswati passed away one night in November 2010, whilst resting in his little *kutir*, at Swargashram Trust kutiya 54, situated between Lakshman Jhoola and Swargashram.

The day his body was discovered, they gave his body to the Ganges.

He was not known to have been suffering from any illness.

More information about Dandi Swami Naryananand Saraswati is available on his web pages; where there are colour photographs, sound recordings and video.

Further information is available about Shankaracharya Swami Brahmanand Saraswati.

www.paulmason.info

CPSIA information can be obtained at www.ICGtesting.com
Printed in the USA
BVOW10s0911160615

404832BV00001B/1/P

9 780956 222848